Build Your Own Computer
From Scratch

Richard (Dick) Whipple

1

Build Your Own Computer – From Scratch

Richard (Dick) Whipple
Visit my website at www.whippleway.com

Printed in the United States of America

First Printing: June 2019
Amazon Kindle (Paperback)

ISBN 978-1-071-25229-1

Contents

Preface

When I first began thinking about this project, I mentioned the idea of building a computer from scratch to an acquaintance. His response was that his twelve-year-old nephew builds computers all the time, so what's the big deal. I explained that I meant really from "scratch" starting with the first principles, AND, OR, and NOT logic. That didn't help. He just looked at me quizzically and moved on to another subject.

I put the Build Your Own Computer (BYOC) idea aside for a while then one day, while exploring computer design ideas on the internet, I came across mention of a software application called Logisim. It was a logic simulator widely used in teaching beginning computer science students. Its graphical user interface and schematic-based design approach were perfect for experimenting with my BYOC ideas.

Using Logisim, I spent several months creating and experimenting with logic circuits based solely on AND, OR, and NOT logic. Eventually I successfully simulated a minimal 10-bit Central Processing Unit (CPU). This was a good first step in proving my BYOC idea was possible. After a couple of months fine tuning the 10-bit CPU design, I began work on a more elaborate 20-bit CPU. This was to become the BYOC CPU described in this book.

I spent several weeks running a series of test programs and troubleshooting problems. It was about this time I grew tired of hand coding programs and created a machine code assembler using Excel. With this time saving addition, I wrote more elaborate programs letting my PC do the translation to machine code. Conway's Game of Life was the culmination of this stage of development.

While pleased with my progress, it was time to begin work on a hardware implementation of the BYOC CPU. Clearly, hand wiring with logic gates was not practical. Again, the internet came to the rescue leading me to a device called a Field Programable Gate Array or FPGA. Using a FPGA, I could program the CPU's logic in a FPGA without physically wiring a single connection.

I had a couple of false starts with FPGAs, then I purchased an Intel Cyclone V GX Starter Kit and downloaded Quartus Lite, the free companion design software. The feature that attracted me to Quartus was its robust schematic design feature. With it, I could directly enter my Logisim schematic design.

After entering the BYOC CPU design in Quartus, I repeated the series of tests developed for the Logisim simulation. Several hurdles including a moderate learning curve with Quartus kept me busy for another few months. In the end, the FPGA implementation was successful, and my working computer became a reality. The day it ran my Life program so fast I had to slow the CPU down to display it properly was the proudest moment I've experienced in many years.

In this book, I begin with first principles (AND, OR, and NOT logic) and carry out a basic computer design finishing with a working computer using a FPGA. A knowledge of computer science or electronics is not needed to follow along. Each step relies on supplied information and simple reasoning.

Though organized by chapters, this book can be further divided into three sections. Chapters 1 to 4 provide theory based on AND, OR, and NOT logic followed by development of the devices needed to build a computer. Chapters 5 to 10 describe and test the simulated version of the BYOC computer design. The remaining chapters, 11 and 12, cover the actual hardware implementation of the computer design in a Field Programmable Gate Array.

While the entire book is written to be accessible to almost anyone, the first eight chapters can be followed, and the computer simulated with a minimum of effort and expense. Chapters 9 and 10, the FPGA implementation, carry some expense (less than $150 as of this writing) and are more challenging though not out of reach for the serious reader.

Lastly, to aid the reader in following the chapter details, additional information, updates, downloads of designs, and software are available on my website http://www.whippleway.com.

Chapter 1 - First Principles

To investigate the concepts of AND, OR, and NOT, consider the physical analogy of water flowing out of a tank through a pipe.

On the left, water flows through the pipe unimpeded and discharges at the end. On the right, a closed valve marked by an "X" stops the flow. If the valve were to open, water would flow again. The table below describes this behavior.

Input Valve	Output Flow
Closed	Off
Open	On

The left column lists all possible "input" conditions while the right column indicates the "output" resulting from each. In this example, "input" is the status of the valve, either "Closed" or "Open". The "output" is water flow, either "Off" or "On".

Except for the physical properties, the table above is the same as the *truth table* used in logic design. To convert the table above to a truth table, replace the physical properties with numeric values "0"and "1", assigning "0" to "Closed/Off" and "1" to "Open/On".

Logical Buffer	
Input	Output
A	Q
0	0
1	1

This truth table describes a *logical buffer*. The term "buffer" reflects that its output is the same as its input but is not connected directly to it.

Logical AND

Adding a second valve downstream as shown modifies the logical behavior and produces a logical AND.

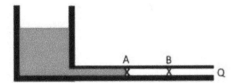

Clearly, both valves A and B must be open to allow flow. This behavior is described in the table below.

Logical AND		
Input	Input	Output
A	B	Q
Closed	Closed	Off
Open	Closed	Off
Closed	Open	Off
Open	Open	On

As before, the Input columns show all possible input conditions and the Output column shows the corresponding output for each. Replacing the

11

physical properties with 0s and 1s transforms it to the truth table for *Logical AND*. The AND's identifying behavior is this: its output is "1" if and only if all inputs are "1".

Logical AND		
Input A	Input B	Output Q
0	0	0
0	1	0
1	0	0
1	1	1

Logical OR

By further rearrangement of the valves and piping, "OR" logic is demonstrated. See the figure below.

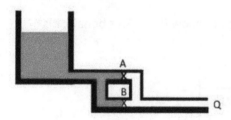

Opening either or both valves will result in water flow. Skipping the "physical properties" step this time, the *logical OR* truth table is shown below.

Logical OR		
Input A	Input B	Output Q
0	0	0
0	1	1
1	0	1
1	1	1

The logical OR's identifying behavior is this: its output is "1" if any or all its inputs are "1".

Logical NOT

NOT logic is the third and last. In the figure below, valves and piping are rearranged as shown.

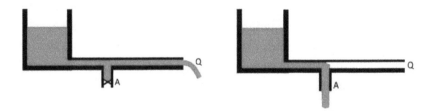

With the valve closed, water flows out the end. Opening the valve, water flow is diverted out the bottom cutting off end flow. In this case a closed valve causes flow, which is the inverse of logical buffer. This inverted behavior is referred to as a *logical NOT*. The corresponding truth table is shown below.

13

Logical NOT	
Input A	Output Q
0	1
1	0

Logic Devices

Below are symbols that represent logic devices that implement the truth tables described above.

| Buffer | AND Gate | OR Gate | NOT Gate or Inverter |

It is not necessary to understand the inner workings (electrical or otherwise) of these devices, just that their output relates to their inputs as described by the corresponding truth table. The same will be true for symbols of additional complex devices developed later.

The output of a NOT is the inverse of the input; a "0" becomes a "1" and vice versa. For this reason, the NOT device is usually referred as an *inverter*. I will use that terminology.

The actual logic symbol for inversion is the small circle at the tip of the logical buffer symbol. Using a small circle to indicate inversion is common practice in digital design.

Logic devices are often called "gates". The term "gate" comes from the way some devices like the AND gate control the flow of "1" and "0" logic data on their inputs. Consider the AND truth table below.

Logical AND		
Input A	Input B	Output Q
0	0	0
0	1	0
1	0	0
1	1	1

If A input is "1", logic data (a "1" or "0") that appears on input B also appears at output Q. If A is "0", Q is always "0" blocking logic data from B. This action is like a "gate" with input A the "gate keeper" controlling the flow of logic data from B to Q.

Buffers and inverters have only one input. AND and OR gates can have two or more inputs. As an example, the AND gate below has three inputs. The accompanying truth table expands the number of inputs to three while maintaining the AND gate's identifying behavior: the output is "1" if and only if all inputs are "1".

3 input AND Gate			
Input A	Input B	Input C	Output Q
0	0	0	0
0	0	1	0
0	1	0	0
0	1	1	0
1	0	0	0
1	0	1	0
1	1	0	0
1	1	1	1

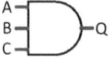

3-Input AND Gate

The figure below shows an OR gate expanded to three inputs.

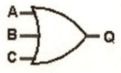

3-Input OR Gate

3 Input OR Gate			
Input A	Input B	Input C	Output Q
0	0	0	0
0	0	1	1
0	1	0	1
0	1	1	1
1	0	0	1
1	0	1	1
1	1	0	1
1	1	1	1

Again, the basic identifying behavior of OR gates is preserved: output Q is "1" if any or all inputs are "1".

In chapter 2, I use Logisim to simulate and test AND, OR, and NOT devices.

Chapter 2 - Logisim

Introducing Logisim

Logisim is a popular logic simulator with an easy-to-use graphical user interface that makes it the perfect tool for developing and testing logic devices and circuits. Logisim can be downloaded free of charge from www.Soundforge.net.

Consider the figure below.

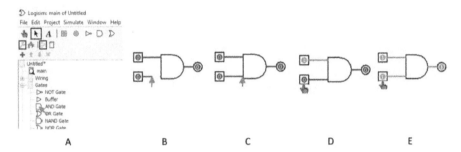

| A | B | C | D | E |

Logisim provides a workspace into which logic devices such as the AND gate in figure A can be dragged and dropped as in figure B. Logic inputs (small squares) and outputs (small circles) can be added to the design in a similar way. Wires connecting components can be added by dragging from contact to contact with the mouse and cursor as in figures B and C. A poke tool (small pointing finger) flips an input from "0" to "1" or vice versa. Note in figures D and E that changing the AND gate's second input to "1" causes the output to change to "1". Note also that dark green (or black) wires indicate a "0" logic level and bright green (or gray) wires indicate a "1" logic level.

Many video tutorials can be found on the internet. Most include helpful examples and cover troubleshooting techniques.

The AND, OR, and NOT circuits below were created with Logisim. By applying all possible input conditions, the figures show that each Logisim logic device produces an output consistent with its truth table.

Logical AND		
Input	Input	Output
A	B	Q
0	0	0
0	1	0
1	0	0
1	1	1

Logical OR		
Input	Input	Output
A	B	Q
0	0	0
0	1	1
1	0	1
1	1	1

NOT Gate	
Input	Output
A	Q
0	1
1	0

In Chapter 3, I develop more complex devices using these AND, OR, and NOT Logisim devices.

Chapter 3 – Combinational Logic

Using only AND, OR, and NOT logic it is possible to develop other, more complex logic devices needed to design a computer. These devices fall into two categories: (1) combinational logic and (2) sequential logic. A combinational logic device's output is purely a function of its current input values. AND, OR, and NOT devices are of this type. A sequential logic device's output depends on its current <u>and</u> past input values. Said another way, sequential logic has the capacity to "remember" while combinational logic does not.

Combinational devices are used extensively in computer design to perform decoding, calculation, and other functions. Listed below are the combinational logic devices developed in this chapter. In each case, only AND, OR, and NOT logic is used to develop the new device. Once developed, a standard symbol will be assigned to the device for future design work.

1. NAND (Not AND) gate
2. NOR (NOT OR) gate
3. XOR (exclusive-or) gate
4. Multiplexer
5. Demultiplexer
6. Decoder
7. Full adder
8. Full subtractor

1. NAND Gate

A *NAND gate* is an AND gate with inverted output; that is, it is a device whose output is "0" when all inputs are "1". See the truth table and symbols below.

NAND Gate		
Input A	Input B	Output Q
0	0	1
0	1	1
1	0	1
1	1	0

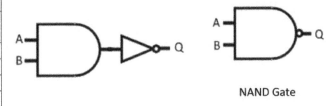

NAND Gate

As shown in the figure, a NAND gate is constructed by inserting an inverter in the AND gate's output. The NAND gate symbol incorporates the inversion circle in the output of an AND gate symbol.

Below is verification of the Logisim NAND gate by truth table above.

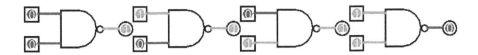

The NAND gate's role in computer design is highly significant. First, all logic functions can be accomplished using only NAND gates. This is called functional completeness. I could have started my quest to build a computer using only NAND gates instead of AND, OR, and NOT gates. Second, the NAND gate is easiest to make using electronic components and therefore lends itself to manufacture. For that reason, the NAND gate has played a prominent role in the history of computers. In my own experience, the first and most often used *integrated circuit gate* was the 7400 chip, a quad 2-input NAND gate. Most of the logic circuits I designed relied heavily on NAND gates. I rarely used a AND gate and when I did, I inverted the output of a spare NAND gate!

This is a good time to introduce the concept of positive and negative logic. In logic design, actions can be initiated by either a logic "1" or "0". When a logic "1" initiates an action, associated inputs and outputs are said to be active high. High active designs are classified as positive logic. If, on the other hand, logic "0" initiates action in the design, the terms used are active low and negative logic design.

Historically, most digital designs were negative logic because of the wide use of readily available NAND-based logic devices. Since we are not constrained by traditional dependence on NAND gate devices, our computer design will be based on positive logic and use AND gates predominately. Personally, I prefer working with positive logic because I think of logic "1" as True and the instigator of an action.

2. NOR Gate

Inverting the output of the OR gate makes a NOR gate. As shown in the NOR gate truth table below, its output is "0" if any or all of its inputs are "1".

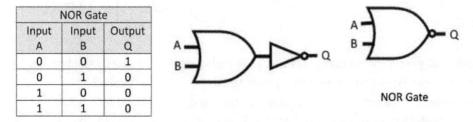

NOR Gate		
Input A	Input B	Output Q
0	0	1
0	1	0
1	0	0
1	1	0

NOR Gate

Like the NAND example, the NOR gate is implemented by inverting the OR's output with an inverter. The Logisim NOR gate symbol above incorporates the inversion circle into the OR gate symbol. Testing the Logisim version of NOR gate yields these correct results.

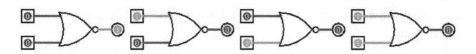

3. Exclusive OR – XOR Gate

Another useful device is the XOR (exclusive-or) gate. Its truth table is given below.

22

XOR Gate			
Row	Input A	Input B	Output Q
1	0	0	0
2	0	1	1
3	1	0	1
4	1	1	0

Observed that the XOR gate's output is "1" if only if the inputs are different. This is the XOR gates identifying behavior.

NAND/NOR gate development was straightforward; we simply inverted AND/OR gate outputs. Developing the XOR gate is not as simple. Happily, a technique called *sum of products* is available to develop it. Here is how it works.

Given a truth table, take note of rows with an output of "1" and ignore "0" rows. For each "1" row, assign the truth table inputs to an AND gate's inputs. If the row's input is "0", insert an inverter in the AND input. Then, connect all AND gate outputs to an OR gate with a suitable number of inputs. The OR gate's output is the Q output of the truth table.

Referring to the XOR truth table, rows 2 and 3 have "1" outputs. On the left below are the two "sum of products" AND gates associated with these rows.

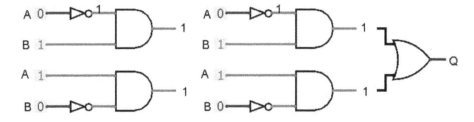

For row 2, the A input is "0", so an inverter is inserted as shown on the right. Likewise, for row 3, an inverter is inserted before the B input. An OR gate combines the AND gate's outputs completing XOR implementation.

Shown below are the four possible input combinations for the XOR circuit with the resulting outputs. They match the XOR truth table exactly!

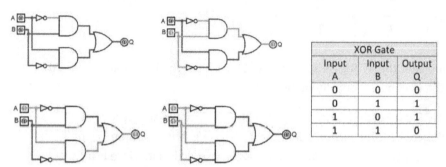

XOR Gate		
Input A	Input B	Output Q
0	0	0
0	1	1
1	0	1
1	1	0

The figure below shows the XOR gate truth table, Logisim AND/OR gate implementation, and symbol.

XOR Gate		
Input A	Input B	Output Q
0	0	0
0	1	1
1	0	1
1	1	0

XOR Gate

Logisim device inputs can be inverted saving the use of separate inverters. Small circles in the middle figure indicate where inverted inputs have replaced inverters in the XOR implementation. Inverting inputs in this way comes in handy as the "sum of products" developed logic circuits grow more complex.

While clearly defining the behavior of logic devices, the truth table is not a compact or convenient form for manipulating logical relationships. *Boolean algebra* is a branch of mathematics that provides a much better approach. For instance, the Boolean expression for an XOR gate is Q = A'·B + A·B' where the plus sign "+" represents the OR operator; a raised dot ".", the AND operator; and the apostrophe "'", the NOT operation. The equation is read, "Q equals A-not and B or A and B-not." Like in regular algebra, A and B are independent variables and Q is the dependent variable. Boolean algebra establishes rules to manipulate logic expressions much as is done with ordinary algebraic expressions.

From Boolean Algebra we get the *operator* terminology for AND, OR, and NOT logic as used above. These *operate* on logic values called operands like A and B. The same goes for ordinary math where addition, subtraction, etc. are also considered operators. We will use this terminology extensively in the work to come.

By the way, the Boolean XOR expression A'·B + A·B' gives a clue as to where the term "sum of products" comes from. Associating the plus sign "+" with an arithmetic "sum" and the raised dot "." with an arithmetic "product", the XOR Boolean expression A' . B + A . B' looks like a "sum" of "products".

4. Multiplexer

The *multiplexer* selects its output from two or more inputs. Consider the simple 2-to-1 multiplexer shown below.

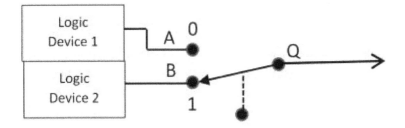

It has three inputs: two logic inputs A and B and one select input S. Its single output is Q. If S is "0", input A and Logic Device 1 are connected to Q. If S is

"1" (as shown), input B and Logic Device 2 are connected to Q. Thus, the 1-bit selector input S controls which of two logic devices connects to the multiplexer's output Q. Shown on the left below is the 2-to-1 multiplexer's truth table.

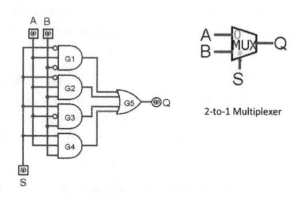

Two-Way Multiplexer			
Input S	Input A	Input B	Output Q
0	0	0	0
0	0	1	0
0	1	0	1
0	1	1	1
1	0	0	0
1	0	1	1
1	1	0	0
1	1	1	1

2-to-1 Multiplexer

All combinations of inputs S, A, and B are listed along with the output for each. Note that when selection code S is "0", Q matches A input ignoring B and when S is "1", Q matches B input ignoring A. Alongside the truth table is the sum of products circuit derived from it. On the right is the Logisim symbol for a multiplexer[1].

In general, the number of selection options equals 2·n where n is the width in bits of the selection code. For the multiplexer above, n is 1 so the number of selection options is 2^1 or 2. A multiplexer with a 3-bit select input accommodates $2^3 = 8$ logic inputs. Logisim provides multiplexer simulations up to 5-bits wide or $2^5 = 32$ logic inputs.

Logisim multiplexers have an optional "enable" input that forces the output Q to either "0" or floating when "0". *Floating* means the output is in effect disconnected. This allows multiple multiplexer outputs to be connected to a single input with only one enabled at a time. Enabling is a useful feature in

---

[1] From this point on I will leave verifying the circuits with Logisim up to you. Doing so is good practice for the work to come.

situations where the status of a single bit overrides the selection of multiple inputs.

5. Demultiplexer

The counterpart to a multiplexer is a *demultiplexer*. It has one input that connects to one of several outputs as determined by a select input. See the figure of a 1-to-2 demultiplexer below.

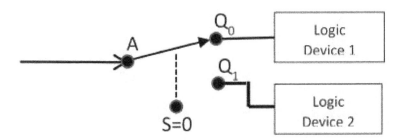

It has two inputs: one logic input A and one selector input S. It has two outputs Q_0 and Q_1. If S is 0 (as shown}, the input A is connected to output Q_0 and Logic Device 1. If S is 1, input A is connected to Q_1 and Logic Device 2.

The approach to implementing the demultiplexer is a variation of the sum of products technique. First, create a truth table for each output, then apply the sum of products technique to each. 1-to-2 demultiplexer truth tables are shown below for each output.

Demultiplexer		
Input S	Input A	Output Q_0
0	0	0
0	1	1
1	0	0
1	1	0

Demultiplexer		
Input S	Input A	Output Q_1
0	0	0
0	1	0
1	0	0
1	1	1

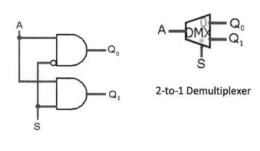

2-to-1 Demultiplexer

With only a single "1" row in each truth table, no OR gate is needed. The demultiplexer's AND gate implementation and equivalent Logisim symbol are as shown.

As with the multiplexer, the number of selection inputs is expandable beyond two. The same rule applies; the number of selectable outputs equals 2^n where n is the number of select bits. A four-way (4 to 1) demultiplexer has a 2-bit selector since $2^2=4$.

6. Decoder

As will become apparent shortly, computers rely on instruction codes to select logic sources, to designate logic destinations, and to initiate actions. The decoder is the device that often makes these selections. For positive logic, the decoder is configured using the sum of products technique and AND gates. The data source for the codes is connected to the select inputs. The output that is "1" indicates which code is present. For negative logic, all is the same except NAND gates are used instead.

Suppose a 2-bit code is to be decoded. As with the demultiplexer, the 2^n rule applies. A 2-bit wide select input (n=2) will provide for four outputs ($2^2=4$). By using AND gates, the selected logic output is "1". This 4-wide decoder truth table and sum of products implementation is shown below.

Four-Way Decoder					
Input S_1	Input S_0	Output Q_0	Output Q_1	Output Q_2	Output Q_3
0	0	1	0	0	0
0	1	0	1	0	0
1	0	0	0	1	0
1	1	0	0	0	1

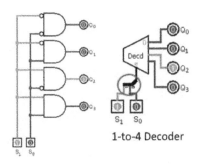

1-to-4 Decoder

The select option shown is code "10". On the right is the equivalent Logisim symbol decoder. As shown, output Q2 is logic "1" when S1="1" and S0="0"[2].

Note that the select input of the decoder is 2-bits wide and denoted by the thick black line. Also shown is a Logisim device called a "splitter" (circled) that combines the separate outputs S1 and S0 into a 2-bit wide *data bus*. Combining and splitting logic wiring avoids the complication of showing multiple parallel wires in the circuit. Imagine the cluttered appearance of a 16-bit data bus if shown as individual wires.

Also, note that the "0" at the top of the logic symbol indicates which output is associated with a "00" select input. The remaining inputs increase in count moving down as shown.

For this project, data bus names use this convention: *name[MSB..LSB]* where *name* is the data bus name; MSB is the most significant bit number of the bus; and LSB is the least significant bit of the bus. For example, the 2-bit

---

[2] Decoders can be designed to support both active high and active low logic.

wide bus above is denoted as S[1..0]. S1 is associated the MSB of S[1..0] and S0 with the LSB.

This notation is very flexible. For example, take a 5-bit bus W[4..0]. To designate only the most significant three bits, write W[4..2]. A single bit such as the MSB would be W[4].

7. Full Adder

The calculating heart of a computer is the Arithmetic-Logic Unit or ALU for short. The logic gates developed so far are useful in designing the "logic" side of the ALU. The basic device needed on the ALU's "Arithmetic" side is the full adder. Using only the full adder, other arithmetic operations can be performed including addition, subtraction, multiplication, and division.

Many of the concepts and techniques used in binary arithmetic are identical to decimal arithmetic except the number system is different. Instead of the ten digits 0 through 9, there are only two: 0 and 1. For instance, counting from 0 to 15 in binary looks like this:

Decimal	0	1	2	3	4	5	6	7	8	9	10	11	12	13	14	15
Binary	0	1	10	11	100	101	110	111	1000	1001	1010	1011	1100	1101	1110	1111

After "1" cannot be "2" as there is no "2" in binary. Instead, adding 1 carries over to the next position as "10". Think of the old joke, "There are only 10 types of people; those that understand binary and those that don't."

Addition follows the same rules as decimal except the sum and carries must be written in terms of 0s and 1s. Here is the example of adding two one-digit binary numbers.

$$A + B = Q$$
$$0 + 0 = 0$$
$$0 + 1 = 1$$

$1 + 0 = 1$

$1 + 1 = 10$ or 0 plus a carry 1

Capturing this as a truth table yields a half adder.

Half Adder			
Input A	Input B	Output Q	Output Carry
0	0	0	0
0	1	1	0
1	0	1	0
1	1	0	1

It is called half adder because it lacks the carry-in capability. More about that shortly. The portion of the truth table covering A, B, and Q should look familiar; it is the same as the XOR gate. The top part of a half-adder is therefore simply an XOR gate. See the figure below.

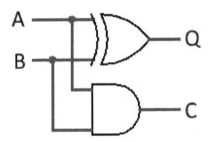

Applying the sum of products technique, the Carry output is implemented adding a single AND gate as shown.

Just as in decimal addition, adding multidigit numbers requires the capability of adding carry-in from the previous column. Including carry-in capability, the half adder becomes a full adder. The full adder truth table looks like this.

Full Adder				
Carry In C_{in}	Input A	Input B	Output Q	Carry Out C_o
1	0	0	0	0	0
2	0	0	1	1	0
3	0	1	0	1	0
4	0	1	1	0	1
5	1	0	0	1	0
6	1	0	1	0	1
7	1	1	0	0	1
8	1	1	1	1	1

As shown in the figure below, full adder output Q is simply the sum of (1) inputs A and B (the output of XOR 1) and (2) carry-in C_{in}.

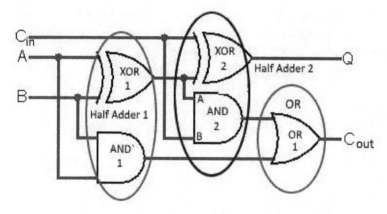

Cout is more complicated. Lines 4 and 8 above indicate that C_o is "1" whenever inputs A and B are both "1" regardless of C_{in}. AND gate 1 supplies this result. Lines 6 and 7 produce a "1" whenever C_{in} is "1" and A and B inputs are different (i.e., A XOR B). AND gate 2 detects this situation with C_{in} connected to input A and the output of XOR gate 1 connected to input B. ORing AND gates 1 and 2 outputs then produces the required C_{out}.

The full adder truth table and Logisim symbol are shown below.

Full Adder				
Input C_{in}	Input A	Input B	Output Q	Output C_{out}
0	0	0	0	0
0	0	1	1	0
0	1	0	1	0
0	1	1	0	1
1	0	0	1	0
1	0	1	0	1
1	1	0	0	1
1	1	1	1	1

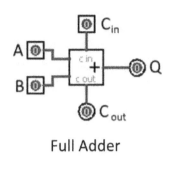

Full Adder

In the figure below, two full adders are connected to add two 2-digit binary numbers, 2 and 3.

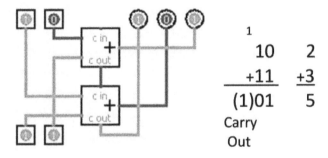

$$
\begin{array}{cc}
1 & \\
10 & 2 \\
+11 & +3 \\
\hline
(1)01 & 5 \\
\end{array}
$$

Carry
Out

The carry-out of the 1s digit is connected to the carry-in of the 2s digit. The carry-out of the 2s digit is available to connect to third full adder to add a 4s digit and so forth.

Thus far logic devices have been designed for single bit inputs and outputs. To build a useful computer, bit widths greater than one are required. Modern computers commonly utilize 32 or even 64-bit width designs. Imagine the nightmare trying to show the wiring of 32 single-bit adders to add two 32-bit values.

Fortunately, design tools like Logisim provide a way to simplify multi-bit logic. As already noted, Logisim "bundles" multi-bit wiring into data buses showing them as heavy black lines. In a similar way, Logisim bundles inputs and outputs of its logic devices, in effect, making them multibit.

For example, the Logisim 4-bit full adder shown below acts as a single device when adding 4-bit bus values A[3..0] and B[3..0] to produce the sum, 4-bit output Q[3..0].

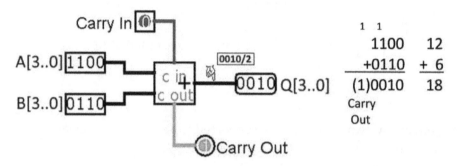

As shown, to read a bus value, hover Logisim's Poke Tool over the bundle and left-click the mouse. The carry-in input to the first adder and carry out output from the fourth adder are 1-bit and colored dark (black) and light green (gray) indicating logic "0" and "1" respectively.

All logic gates and devices discussed so far can be configured as multi-bit. For instance, the 8-bit configured AND gate below ANDs together two 8-bit values.

A[7..0] 10101010 ──┐
)──── 00001010 Q[7..0]
B[7..0] 00001111 ──┘

```
  10101010 A[7..0]
AND 00001111 B[7..0]
  00001010 Q[7..0]
```

Note that the AND is *bit wise*; that is, each bit of A[7..0] is ANDed with the corresponding bit of B[7..0] to produce the corresponding bits output Q[7..0]. Bit wise applies similarly other gates and logic devices when appropriate.

8. Full Subtractor

As suggested earlier, subtraction can be accomplished with a full adder. However, a full subtractor is not that different from a full adder. Following the approach above but with the half subtractor instead of half adder, produces the logic circuit below.

Half Subtractor (A - B)			
Input A	Input B	Output Q	Output Borrow
0	0	0	0
0	1	1	1
1	0	1	0
1	1	0	0

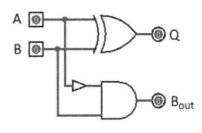

The only difference between the half-added and half-subtractor is the inverter in the A circuit of the borrow AND gate. Output Q is still an exclusive-or of A and B. Borrow-out by sum of products is an AND gate with the A input inverted. The full subtractor truth table is shown below.

	Full Subtractor (A - B)				
	Input Bin	Input A	Input B	Output Q	Output Bout
1	0	0	0	0	0
2	0	0	1	1	1
3	0	1	0	1	0
4	0	1	1	0	0
5	1	0	0	1	1
6	1	0	1	0	1
7	1	1	0	0	0
8	1	1	1	1	1

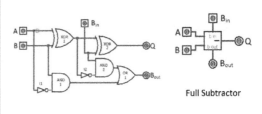

Full Subtractor

Output Q is the difference of (A-B) and Bin and is produced by connecting the output of XOR 1 to one input of XOR 2 and Bin to the other. As for Bout, its output is "1" when A is "0" and B is "1" (lines 2 and 6) and when A and B are the same and Bin in "1" (lines 5 and 8). AND gates 1 and 2 detect these conditions, then OR gate 1 combines their outputs to produce Bout.

The development of combination logic needed to build a computer is complete. Here again is a list.

> AND gate
> OR gate
> Inverter (NOT)
> NAND (Not AND) gate
> NOR (NOT OR) gate
> XOR (exclusive-or) gate
> Multiplexer
> Demultiplexer
> Decoder
> Full adder
> Full subtractor

Keep in mind that these logic devices have no memory capability. Once input values are applied, the output is strictly determined by the device's truth table. If an input changes, the output changes according to the truth table without any relationship to the previous input values.

In Chapter 4, I develop sequential devices that <u>have memory</u> and outputs that <u>are affected</u> by previous input states.

Chapter 4 – Sequential Logic

Combinational devices have no capacity to "remember". Their output depends only on their current inputs. To build a computer, some devices must remember their input states and change states only at specific times.

Computers rely on a read-process-write capability. For example, suppose two values are read from memory, an arithmetic or logic operation performed on them, and the result stored back in original memory. Obviously, this cannot be done with combinational logic because inputs would change during the calculation voiding the result. To avoid this, tasks carried out during the operation must be "sequenced in time" with intermediate results "remembered" while the result is calculated. Only then can original memory be updated. This sequencing and remembering is the role of sequential logic.

Like combinational logic, sequential logic can be made from AND, OR, and NOT devices. The trick is to use feedback via a path from the gate's output back to its input. Feedback permits a device to maintain an output (either "1" or "0") even if some inputs change. In addition, the output changes only on arrival of a *timing* or *clock pulse*. Thus, feedback gives the device both sequencing and memory capability.

Listed below are the sequential logic devices to be developed.

> D-Type Flip Flop
> Data Register
> Random Access Memory
> Read Only Memory

S-R Flip Flop

The core device for all is the *Flip Flop*. By interconnecting Flip Flops in various ways, data registers and computer memory can be made. The simplest Flip Flop is the Set-Reset or S-R Flip Flop. See the circuit below and accompanying truth table.

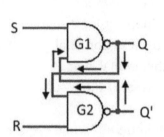

		S-R Flip Flop			
#	Input S	Input R	Output Q	Output Q'	Description
1	1	1	0	1	No Change
2	1-0-1*	1	1	0	Set
3	1	1	1	0	No Change
4	1	1-0-1*	0	1	Reset
5	1	1	1	1	Invalid
6	1	1	0	0	Invalid

* The S(Set) or R(Reset) inputs, normally "1", are driven to "0" momentarily by a negative going clock pulse.

The arrows show the feedback paths between the two NAND gates. With feedback, it is possible to change Q to "1" or "0" timed with a negative going clock pulse on the S or R input, respectively. Once the pulse returns to "1", Q will hold the new value indefinitely. Thus, the circuit exhibits the sequencing and memory capability desired.

To better understand how the S-R Flip Flop works, refer to the truth table above. Assume as in line #1 that S and R inputs are "1", output Q is "0", and output Q'(read Q NOT) is "1". With S and R both "1", this is a stable configuration, in effect "remembering" the Q is "0" and alternately, Q' is "1". If S input drops to zero momentarily, as in line 2, NAND gate G1's output Q "flips" to "1" because one of its inputs is now "0". Referring to NAND gate G2, both its inputs are now "1" dropping Q' to "0". Since Q' is connected to the input of G1, Q stays at

"1" even after S returns to "1". Thus, momentarily dropping S to "0" sets (flips) Q to "1" and holds it in fully stable state line #3. In a similar way, lines 3 and 4 of the truth table show how a momentary "0" on the R input resets (flops) Q to "0" and holds it. This setting and resetting (flipping and flopping) gives the circuit the quaint name "S(et)-R(eset) Type Flip Flop".

This is a good time to introduce some new terms. If a device's action takes place on a "1" to "0" transition of a clock pulse, it is said to be *falling edge clocked*. If action occurs on a "0" to "1" transition, the device is *rising edge clocked*. The S-R Flip Flop described above is falling edge clocked.

If the output of a device is "1" after a clocking action, it is said to have been *set*. If "0", it has been *reset*. A falling edge clock on the S input of a R-S Flip Flop sets the output to "1". A clock pulse on the R input, reset its output to "0". From this point on, I use set to mean making the output of a device "1" and reset to make it "0".

The S-R Flip Flop has a potential problem area. Lines 5 and 6 of the truth table above show conditions inconsistent with the behavior of NAND gates. Take line 5 for instance. Q and Q' cannot both be "1" while both R and S are "1" because this would be an invalid state for a NAND gate. Similarly, line 6 shows another invalid state. To get around this, the circuit must be modified to eliminate the possibility of lines 5 and 6 occurring.

1. D-Type Flip Flop

By applying a few modifications, the invalid states of the S-R Flip Flop are eliminated. Consider the modified S-R Flip Flop truth table and circuit below.

Modified S-R Flip Flop						
#	Input C	Input D	Output Y	Output Y'	Output S	Output R
1	0	x	0	0	1	1
2	1	1	1	0	0	1
3	1	0	0	1	1	0

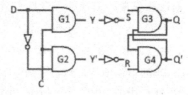

Looking at line #1, while C is "0", S and R are both "1" preventing outputs Q and Q' from changing. This provides the "memory" feature required. If C is "1", the inverter between G1 and G2 inputs ensures that Y and Y' are not both 1. This eliminates the unstable condition in lines 5 and 6 of the S-R Flip Flop. Further, line 2 shows that when C is "1" and D is "1", S drops to "0" setting the output Q of the S-R Flip Flop to "1", matching the value of D. Similarly, line 3 is the case when C is "1" and D is "0" making output Q a "0", again matching D. In either case, when C (the clock) returns to "0", the value of D (the data) is remembered at Q.

In summary, a rising edge clock pulse (0-1-0) on the clock input C transfers the value of the D (Data) input to Q. This modified S-R Flip Flop is called a *D-Type Flip Flop*. It exhibits both sequencing and memory capability without the S-R Flip Flop's invalid states.

On the left of the figure below is the basic Data or D-Type Flip Flop. In the center is a more elaborate version that includes active high enable, set, and reset inputs. On the right is the Logisim symbol.

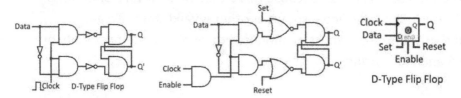

For the Logisim D-Type Flip Flop, there are four clocking options: rising edge, falling edge, high value, or low value. For the Logisim computer design, the rising edge option will be used.

2. Data Register

Computers store and manipulate multibit values. A common choice is 8 bits. To store 8-bit data, eight D-Type Flip Flops are connected in parallel as shown below.

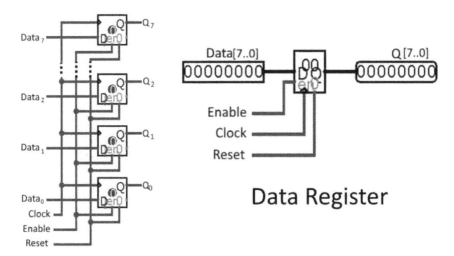

Data Register

This configuration is called a *register*. As indicated, all inputs except for data are connected in parallel. Note that the Logisim device does not include a Set input, only a Reset. Registers of other widths are found in modern computer designs usually storing data in widths that are multiples of eight; for example, 16, 32, and 64 bits. Logisim registers can be configured up to 32 bits wide.

The figure below shows an 8-bit Logisim register before and after arrival of a rising edge clock pulse.

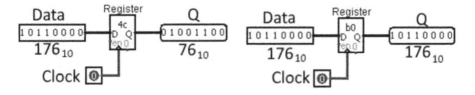

Assume that 76 is the 8-bit data output value Q before the clock pulse and that the data input (176) value is the result of an arithmetic calculation using the output value 76. At the rising edge of the clock pulse, the calculated result 176 moves to the output shown on the right and becomes the new value of Q. As pointed out previously, this clock sequenced, read-process-write capability is crucial to the design of computers.

An important point to note here is that the register held the old value (76) until the write operation is completed. Not all registers and memory devices behave this way. Choosing devices that hold the "old value" until clocked must be used in our design to ensure read-process-write integrity.

3. Random Access Memory (RAM)

Computer *Random Access Memory* or *RAM* consists of data registers organized in multiples-of-two along with control circuitry that selects which register is being accessed. Below is a very basic RAM made from an array of four 8-bit registers. Alongside is the equivalent Logisim implementation.

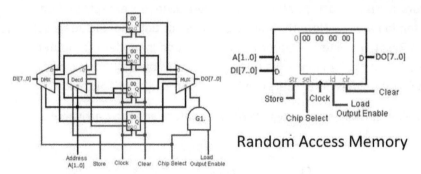

Random Access Memory

Below is a description of its inputs and output.

Inputs:

Address – A 2-bit wide bus input connected to the input of the decoder, multiplexer, and demultiplexer. The address input serves three functions;

namely, (1) selects which register is enabled via the decoder Decd, (2) routes input DI[7..0] to that selected register via the demultiplexer DMX, and (3) connects the selected register to output DO[7..0] via the multiplexer MUX.

Store – Single-bit input connected to the enable input of the decoder forcing all register enable inputs to "0" if it is "0". If Store and Chip Select inputs are "1", a clock pulse on Clock will store the value DI[7..0] to the enabled register.

Clock – Single bit input connected to the register clock inputs. If Chip Select and Store inputs are "1", the rising edge of a clock pulse on Clock will store the value DI[7..0] in the enabled register.

Clear – Single bit input connected to the register clear inputs. If Clear is "1", all register outputs are zeroed regardless of the state of other inputs. This overriding behavior is referred to as asynchronous because it occurs immediately without regard for any synchronous (clock driven) actions of the memory.

Chip Select – Single bit input connected to the enable input of demultiplexer DMX. A "1" on Chip Select enables the demultiplexer providing a pathway for memory input DI[7..0] to the registers. Should a Clock pulse arrive while Chip Select is "1", register output DO[7..0] will update to DI[7..0].

Load/Output Enable – Single bit input connected via AND gate G1 to the enable input of multiplexer MUX. A "1" on both Load/Output Enable and Chip Select inputs enables the multiplexer MUX placing the register output on DO[7..0]. Load/Output Enable is used to expand memory by allowing multiple banks of memory to share a common output bus with only one being enabled at a time. MUX's output circuitry is designed so that when Load/Output Enabled is "0", the Data Output pins are floating; that is, essentially disconnected from the external bus. In this way multiple memory devices can share a common bus with only one enabled at a time. DI[7..0] – 8-bit wide input that, when Chip Select and Store are "1", supplies the value to be stored in the registers.

Output:

DO[7..0] – 8-bit wide output that, when the Chip Select and Load/Output Enable are "1", reflects the registers output. Logisim random access memory or RAM offers optional data widths up to 32 bits and 224 or 16,777,216 addressable memory locations!

In a typical computer application RAM is used to store large amounts of data. Access is achieved by placing the address of the data on the Address Input then using the remaining inputs to read or write to the addressed register (sometimes called a *location*).

4. Read Only Memory (ROM)

Read Only Memory or ROM differs from RAM in that it is non-volatile; that is, it retains its memory even without power applied. Computer instructions (the program) are stored in ROM so that they execute on power up. ROM address and chip selection circuitry is generally the same as RAM with the exception that Data or Store circuitry is not needed.

Since each ROM memory output bit is fixed as either a "0" or "1", it need not implemented with a D-Type Flip Flop. Actual ROM design is not covered here because the approaches vary widely depending on the application. Some types are permanently programmed at manufacture; some are programmed only once after manufacture; still others can be erased and programmed multiple times.

Logisim's ROM component is shown below.

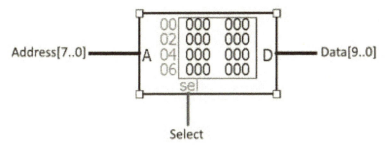

Address[7..0] ——— A 00 000 000 D ——— Data[9..0]
                     02 000 000
                     04 000 000
                     06 000 000
                         sel

Select

Read Only Memory

Like Logisim RAM, the ROM can be configured in optional data word widths up to 32 bits and can address up to 224 or 16,777,216 memory locations. The ROM shown is configured as 256 10-bit instruction words. It can be programmed using the keyboard, typing one byte at the time, or loaded from a specially formatted file. More about this later when it comes time to write and test a program.

This completes development of all the logic devices required to build our computer. Here's the list.

Combination Devices:

> AND gate
> OR gate
> Inverter (NOT gate)
> NAND (Not AND) gate
> NOR (NOT OR) gate
> XOR (exclusive-or) gate
> Multiplexer
> Demultiplexer
> Decoder
> Full adder
> Full subtractor

> Sequential Devices:

D-Type Flip Flop
Data Register
Random Access Memory
Read Only Memory

In the next chapter, I develop specifications for the computer.

Chapter 5 – BYOC CPU Specification

Computer Architecture

Computer architecture varies widely depending on the end use. Without an application in mind, the best choice for the BYOC computer is to use the general-purpose architecture illustrated in the block diagram below.

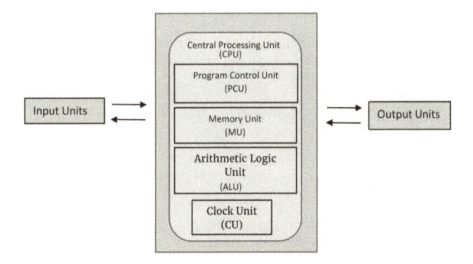

The Central Processing Unit (CPU) consists of these units:

Program Control Unit (PCU) – The PCU's primary function is to control CPU operation based on instruction words stored in its Read-Only-Memory (ROM). Normally, instructions are executed one after the other from consecutive ROM addresses. For branch/jump/call instructions, the PUC may redirect execution to another ROM address depending on a condition existing from previous instructions.

Memory Unit (MU) – All data storage requirements are met with the MU. This is accomplished with general purpose registers and Random Access Memory (RAM). Registers are manipulated directly using instructions in

47

ROM. RAM is accessed indirectly by address and used for primarily for data storage.

Arithmetic Logic Unit (ALU) – The ALU performs arithmetic and logic operations as indicated by instructions in ROM. The ALU operator is coded in the instruction word. Operands come from data in the MU and the instruction word. The ALU result is passed back to the MU for storage.

Clock Unit (CU) – The CU creates the clock timing pulses that control sequencing in other units. INPUT & OUTPUT Units (INU & OUTU)– Provide the interface between the CPU and external units.

External to the CPU are **Input** and **Output Units** such as keyboards, displays, controllers, sensors, etc. These provide an interface between the CPU and the real world.

Below are BYOC CPU specifications based on this architecture.

BYOC CPU Specifications

Instruction Format - Single 20-bit instruction word.
Random Access Memory (Data RAM) for Data Storage - 16-bits wide up to 65,536 bytes used to store data.
Read Only Memory (Program ROM) for Program Storage: 20 bits wide up to 65,536 bytes used to store program instructions.
Arithmetic and Logic Operators – As follows:

> Add two 8-bit values
> Add two 8-bit values with a carry
> Subtract two 8-bit values
> Subtract two 8-bit values with a borrow
> Compare two 8-bit values
> Increment register
> Decrement register

Bitwise AND two 8-bit values

Bitwise OR two 8-bit values

Bitwise XOR (exclusive or) two 8-bit values

Bitwise NOT (inversion) of an 8-bit value

Rotate register left to carry (0 rotated to least significant bit of register)

Rotate register right (0 rotated to most significant bit of register)

Rotate register left through carry (carry rotated to least significant bit of register)

Rotate register right through carry (carry rotated to most significant bit of register)

Push register on to stack memory

Pop register off stack memory

Input to register from external port

Output register to external port

Additional operations up to a total of sixty-four maximum

General Purpose Registers - Seven 8-bit registers designated A, B, C, D, E, H, and L.

Status Bit Registers - Two 1-bit registers designated Zero and Carry. Each indicates a zero and/or carry result from the last ALU operation. For example, if a subtraction results in a zero, the Zero status bit is set to "1". If an addition results in a carry, the Carry status bit is set to "1". Otherwise, status bits are "0". Not all operations affect status bits. See the "Register Based Instructions" section below.

RAM Access - An 8-bit memory register designated M provides read and write access to Data RAM locations specified by an address in the HL registers (most significant byte of address in H).

ROM Access - An 8-bit value in ROM can be loaded into a register using a move immediate instruction or can be read from ROM with an address in the DE registers (most significant byte of address in D). Write operation to the ROM is prohibited.

Conditional branch - Change program execution address based on a condition). Branch Conditions include an ALU result of zero, not zero, carry,

49

and no carry. Conditional branching is restricted to within -256 to +255 bytes of the branching instruction's address.

Unconditional jump - Change program execution address without condition either directly via an address that is part of the instruction word or indirectly using the address pointed to by the HL register pair.

Unconditional subroutines - Execute via a call instruction the code at an address that is part of the instruction word. Companion return instruction to change program execution to the address following the associated call instruction.

Push and pop instructions - Instructions that save and restore register values on a stack RAM.

BYOC CPU Instruction Set

Information encoded in the 20-bit instruction word determines the actions the CPU takes in performing given tasks. The coded information falls into three categories:

Instruction Type - BYOC instructions are divided into eight types represented by a 3-bit binary code. The Instruction Type Codes (ttt) are as follows:

Code	Instruction Type
"000"[3]	MVI Move 8-bit immediate value to the destination register.
"001"	RIO Register-immediate value operation. Example: Add a constant to a register.
"010"	MOV Move a 8-bit data value from source register to a destination register.
"011"	LDI Register load indirect from Data ROM or Data RAM at

---

[3] Binary values will be shown in quotation marks such as "100" (4 decimal). Hexadecimal (base 16) numbers will be shown as 0x0A(10 decimal). Decimal numbers will be shown in the usual way like 1024.

address in DE register pair

"100"   RRO   Register-to-register operation. Example: Subtract one register from another.

"101"   BRC   Branch conditional

"110"   CRT   Call/Return

"111"   JIA   Unconditional jump or replace instruction address with HL register pair

Source and Destination Register – The BYOC CPU has eight registers (7 general purpose registers plus memory register M) represented by a 3-bit binary code. The Register Codes (sss/ddd) are listed below:

Code	Register
"000"	B register
"001"	C register
"010"	D register
"011"	E register
"100"	H register
"101"	L register
"110"	M (data memory) register
"111"	A register

ALU Operator – The BYOC CPU supports up to sixty-four ALU operations represented by a 6-bit number, cccccc. The ALU Operation Codes are listed in the "Instruction Set" below.

Instruction codes occupy precisely defined positions in the instruction word. Not all codes appear in all instructions, but when they do, they always occupy the same position. In determining the order of the codes, these are the considerations:

1. Instruction type comes first because it appears in all instructions.
2. The move immediate MVI instruction type has instruction type (ttt), destination register code (ddd), and the 8-bit data value to be moved (loaded) into the destination register, so it makes sense to place

destination register code after instruction type code. Thus far the instruction word looks like this: ttt ddd xx xxxx xxxx xxxx .

3. The register-to-register RRO instruction type includes instruction type (ttt), destination register code (ddd), operation code (cccccc), and source register code (sss). cccccc or sss could be next except that the register-to-immediate RIO type has cccccc but not sss. This suggests that cccccc be next giving the RRO instruction type the final form, ttt ddd cccccc sss xxxxx.

4. The RIO instruction is then ttt ddd cccccc vvvvvvvv allowing for an 8-bit value v..v as part of the register-to-immediate operation.

The 20-bit instruction word as stored in the Program ROM is designated as ROMPrgm[19..0]. The final code positions are as follows:

Instruction Type Code (ttt) - ROMPrgm[19..17]
Destination Register Code (ddd) - ROMPrgm[16..14]
ALU Opcode Code (cccccc) - ROMPrgm[13..8]
Source Register Code (sss) - ROMPrgm[7..5]

Instruction Set

An important part of the BYOC specification is the instruction set defining the instruction words that will carry out computing tasks. The following abbreviations are used in specifying the instruction set:

V, v..v   Constant 8-bit binary data value
A, a..a   Constant 16-bit address
ttt   Type code (see above)
ddd/sss Destination and source register code (see above)
cccccc   ALU operator
l..l c..c   ALU level and code (ccc ccc = l..l c..c)
p   I/O port 0 to 255 ("00000000" to "11111111")
OPC   ALU Operator Code

OP0	ALU Operand 0
OP1	ALU Operand 1
→	Value assigned from source on left to destination on right
ASM	Assembly pneumonic used to provide a more English language form of the instruction
Lbl	Call, jump, or branch destination in assembly code
rs/rd	Source/destination registers by name B, C, D, E, H, L, M, or A
Z	Zero and zero status bit
C	Carry and carry status bit
B	Borrow

The BYOC instruction set is specified below. Entries are by instruction type and include the binary form of the instruction, a description, the assembly code designation, and the status bits affected when the instruction is executed. Not all instructions are defined leaving room for expansion later.

1. MVI Type (ttt=000) – Move Immediate Instruction

000 ddd xxxxxx vvvv vvvv

Description	ASM	Status*	Operation
Move immediate value to register	MVI r_d, V	None	V → r_d

* Status bits affected by the instruction

2. RIO Type (ttt=001) – Register Immediate Operation with constant

001 ddd cccccc vvvv vvvv

cccccc	Description	ASM	Status	Operation
000000	Add immediate	ADI r_d ,v	Z,C	r_d +V → r_d
000001	Add immediate	ACI r_d ,v	Z,C	r_d +V+C → r_d

53

w/ carrry

000010	Subtract immediate	SUI r_d ,v	Z,C	r_d -V $\rightarrow$ r_d
000011	Subtract immediate w/ borrow	SBI r_d ,v	Z,C	r_d -V-B $\rightarrow$ r_d
000100	Compare immediate	CPI r_d ,v	Z,C	r_d - V $\rightarrow$ none*
011000	AND immediate	ANI r_d ,v	Z,C=0	r_d AND V $\rightarrow$ r_d
011001	OR immediate	ORI r_d ,v	Z,C=0	r_d OR V $\rightarrow$ r_d
011010	XOR immediate	XRI r_d ,v	Z, C=0	r_d XOR V $\rightarrow$ r_d

* destination register unaffected by operation

3. MOV Type (ttt=010) – Move Register to Register sss $\rightarrow$ ddd

010 ddd xxxxxx sss xxxxx

Description	ASM	Status	Operation
Move register to register	MOV r_d,r_s	None	$r_s \rightarrow r_d$

4. LDI Type (ttt=011) – Register Load from Data ROM and RAM

011 ddd 0x xxxx xxxx xxxx

Description	ASM	Status	Operation
Load byte to register from Data ROM at address a..a in DE*	LROM r_d	None	$(DE)_{ROM} \rightarrow r_d$

011 ddd 1x xxxx xxxx xxxx

Description	ASM	Status	Operation
Load byte to register from Data RAM at address a..a in DE*	LRAM r_d	None	$(DE)_{RAM} \rightarrow r_d$

* When register pair DE contains an address, D is the high order eight bits and E is the lower.

5. RRO (ttt=100) – Register-to-Register Operation

100 ddd lllccc sss xxxxx

Level 0 (l..l="000") - ALU0

54

c..c	Description	ASM	Status	Operation
000	Add register	ADD r_d,r_s	Z,C	$r_d + r_s \rightarrow r_d$
001	Add register w/ carry	ADC r_d,r_s	Z,C	$r_d + r_s + C \rightarrow r_d$
010	Subtract register	SUB r_d,r_s	Z,C	$r_d - r_s \rightarrow r_d$
011	Subtract w/ borrow	SBB r_d,r_s	Z,C	$r_d - r_s - B \rightarrow r_d$
100	Compare register	CMP r_d,r_s	Z,C	$r_d - r_s \rightarrow$ none*
101	Undefined		Z,C	
110	Undefined		Z,C	
111	Undefined		Z,C	

* r_d unaffected by operation

Level 1 (l..l="001") - ALU1

ccc	Description	ASM	Status	Operation
000	Undefined		Z,C	
001	Undefined		Z,C	
010	Undefined		Z,C	
011	Undefined		Z,C	
100	Undefined		Z,C	
101	Undefined		Z,C	
110	Undefined		Z,C	
111	Undefined		Z,C	

Level 2(l..l="010") - ALU2

ccc	Description	ASM	Status	Operation
000	Increment register	INC r_d	Z	$r_d + 1 \rightarrow r_d$
001	Decrement register	DCR r_d	Z	$r_d - 1 \rightarrow r_d$
010	Increment register on Z	INZ r_d	Z	$r_d + 1 \rightarrow r_d$
011	Decrement register on Z	DCR r_d	Z	$r_d - 1 \rightarrow r_d$
100	Undefined		Z	

101	Undefined		Z
110	Undefined		Z
111	Undefined		Z

Level 3 (I..I="011") - ALU3

ccc	Description	ASM	Status	Operation
000	AND register	AND r_d r_s	Z,C=0	r_d AND r_s → r_d
001	OR register	OR r_d ,r_s	Z,C=0	r_d OR r_s → r_d
010	XOR register	XOR r_d ,r_s	Z,C=0	r_d XOR r_s → r_d
011	NOT register	NOT r_d ,r_s	Z,C=0	NOT(r_s) → r_d
100	Undefined		Z,C=0	
101	Undefined		Z,C=0	
110	Undefined		Z,C=0	
111	Undefined		Z,C=0	

Level 4 (III="100") - ALU4

ccc	Description	ASM	Status	Operation
000	Rotate register left r_d	RLC r_d	C	msb* r_d to C & 0 to lsb*
001	Rotate register right	RRC rd	C	lsb r_d to C & 0 to msb r_d
010	Rotate register left	RAL rd	C	msb r_d to C & C to lsb r_d
011	Rotate register right	RAR rd	C	lsb r_d to C & C to msb r_d
100	Undefined		C	
101	Undefined		C	
110	Undefined		C	
111	Undefined		C	

* msb = most significant bit lsb = least significant bit

Level 5 (I..I="001") – ALU5

ccc	Description	ASM	Status	Operation

ccc		Status
000	Undefined	Z,C
001	Undefined	Z,C
010	Undefined	Z,C
011	Undefined	Z,C
100	Undefined	Z,C
101	Undefined	Z,C
110	Undefined	Z,C
111	Undefined	Z,C

Level 6 (III=110") - ALU6

ccc	Description	ASM	Status	Operation
000	Push r_d on stack	PUSH r_d	None	$r_d \rightarrow (STACK)_{PP}$
001	Output r_d to port p	OUT p,r_d	None	$r_d \rightarrow (PORT)_P$
010	Undefined		None	
111	Undefined		None	
100	Undefined		None	
101	Undefined		None	
110	Undefined		None	
111	Undefined		None	

Level 7 III=111") - ALU7

ccc	Description	ASM	Status	Operation
000	Pop r_d off stack	POP rd	None	$(STACK)_{PP} \rightarrow r_d$
001	Input to r_d from port p	INP rd,p	None	$(PORT)_P \rightarrow r_d$
010	Load r_d from address aaaaa*	LDR rd,A	None	$(A) \rightarrow r_d$
011	Store r_d at address aaaaa**	STR rd,A	None	$r_d \rightarrow (A)$
100	Undefined	None		
101	Undefined	None		
110	Undefined	None		
111	Undefined	None		

* 100 ddd 111 010 aaaaa where aaaaa is 5-bit address (0 to 31)

** 100 ddd 111 011 aaaaa where aaaaa is 5-bit address (0 to 31)

Note: ALU6 and ALU7 are single register operations. Rd is used for both destination and source so that port p can be 8 bits wide.

6. BRC Type (ttt=101) – Branch Conditional

101 x 000 xxxx v vvvv vvvv

Description	ASM	Status
Branch on Zero to PC+v..v	BZ Lbl	None

101 x 001 xxxx v vvvv vvvv

Branch on not Zero to PC+v..v	BNZ Lbl	None

101 x 010 xxxx v vvvv vvvv

Branch on Carry to PC+v..v	BC Lbl	None

101 x 011 xxxx v vvvv vvvv

Branch on no Carry to PC+v..v	BNC Lbl	None

101 x 100 Undefined

101 x 101 Undefined

101 x 110 Undefined

101 x 111 xxxx v vvvv vvvv

Branch unconditional to PC+v..v	BR Lbl	None

Note: In each case v..v is calculated from the current address to the address of the label Lbl. Maximum branching distance is -256 to +255 from Lbl.

7. CRT Type (ttt=110) – Call/Return Unconditional

110 0 xxxx xxxx xxxx xxxx

Description	ASM	Status
Return from call	RET	None

110 1 vvvv vvvv vvvv vvvv

Call unconditional   CALL A   None to a..a (0 to 65,535)

8. JIA Type (ttt=111) – Jump/Replace Instruction Address with HL Unconditional (JIA)

111 0 xxxx xxxx xxxx xxxx

Description	ASM	Status
Jump to address in HL	IAHL	None

111 1 vvvv vvvv vvvv vvvv

Jump to address A   JMP A   None
A = a..a (0 to 65,535)

To get a better idea of how instructions are executed, consider the simple program below that counts down from 5 to 0 in the A register then starts over. Later, it will be used for initial testing of the BYOC CPU.

Address	Instruction	ASM Code	Description
0	000 111 000000 00000001	START: MVI A,1	Move 1 to A. A=1
1	010 010 000000 111 00000	MOV D,A	Move A to D. D=1 and A=1.
2	000 111 000000 00000101	MVI A,5	Move count 5 to A. A=5.
3	100 111 000010 010 00000	LOOP: SUB A,D	Subtract D=1 from A and store in A.
4	101 0 001 0000 111111111	BNZ LOOP	Branch on not zero back 1 to LOOP and subtract D=1 again. When A=0, fall through to line 5.
5	111 1 0000 0000 0000 0000	JMP START	Jump to START and do over

Following is an instruction-by-instruction description of program execution:

Adrs 0 000 111 000000 00000001   MVI A,1   1→A

The first three bits "000" indicate this instruction is type MVI, move immediate to register. The second three bits "111" specify destination register A. The lower 8 bits ("00000001" = 1) is the data to be moved (loaded) into A. After execution, the value stored in A register will be 1.

59

Adrs 1 010 010 000000 111 00000 MOV D,A A→D

"010" is the move instruction type MOV. The source register "111" is A, and the destination register "010" is D. The value in register A is moved (copied) to register D. After execution, the value stored in both A and D will be 1.

Adrs 2 000 111 000000 00000101 MVI A,5 5→A

Again, it is a move immediate type MVI to register A instruction. After execution, the value stored in register A will be 5.

Adrs 3 100 111 000010 010 00000 SUB A,D A-D→A

"100" is a register-to-register operation type RRO. The source (subtrahend) is "010", the D register. The destination (minuend and result) is "111", the A register. The ALU operation is "000010", subtraction without borrow. The value in D (which is 1) is subtracted from the value in A (which is 5), leaving the result 4 in the A. After execution, the value stored in register A will be 4 and in D will be 1 (unchanged).

Adrs 4 101 0 001 0000 111111111 BNZ -1

Branch on not zero back 1 to address 3, otherwise continue to address 5

 "101" is a branch on condition instruction (BRC). Skipping a bit, the next 3-bit grouping "001" identifies it as a conditional branch BNZ, branch on not zero.

The value v..v to be added to the Instruction Address Register is "111111111", the value is in two's complement of -1. Two's complement representation is a bit like a car's odometer. As the odometer rolls forward from 0, numbers increase in a positive since; i.e., 1, 2, 3, and so forth.   When an odometer rolls backwards from 0, it registers 99999 and counts down from there to 99998, 99997, and on and on. Imagine that the number line is imposed on the odometer readings:

Number Line   . . ., 3, 2, 1, 0, -1, -2, -3, . . .
Odometer   . . ., 3. 2. 1. 0, 99999, 99998, 99997, . . .

The positive numbers and zero are the same while the rollover values are interpreted as negative numbers.

Given the 9-bit binary number v..v above, the table below shows the correspondence between two's complement and standard notation values.

Two's Complement	Standard
011111111	255
...	...
000000011	3
000000010	2
000000001	1
000000000	0
111111111	-1
111111110	-2
111111101	-3
...	...
100000000	-256

Note that the left most bit of a two's complement number acts as a sign bit resulting in the loss of one digit in number range. So instead of v..v ranging from 0 to 512, it ranges from -256 to +255. Two's complement numbers provide the capability of branching forward and backward from the current memory address.

Numbers used in computing are referred to as either unsigned and signed, the latter being in two's complement form. For example, if "11111110" is unsigned, it equals 511. If it is signed, then its value is -2.

How the value is interpreted depends on the instruction. For instance, branching instructions treat the number v..v as a signed value -256 to 255 while the CALL and JMP instructions treat a..a as an unsigned value 0 to 64,535.

Adrs 5 111 1 0000 0000 0000 0000   JMP 0

Jump unconditionally to START (address 0x0000).

 The jump's target address is coded as an unsigned number in the right-most 16 bits. After execution, program execution continues at address 0x0000, restarting the program.

The BYOC CPU is now fully specified. In the next chapter I carry out the design.

Chapter 6 – The BYOC CPU Design

Design Constraints

The BYOC CPU design consists of these units: Clock Unit (CU), Program Control Unit (PCU), Memory Unit (MU), and Arithmetic Logic Unit (ALU). In a later chapter, I/O units to interface the CPU to a keyboard, display, and other peripherals will be described. First, I discuss constraints that guided the design.

1. Information codes occupy precise and fixed positions in all instructions. Codes may not appear in all instructions, but when they do, they conform to this constraint. The bit position of information codes in the instruction word ROMPrgm[19..0] are as follows:

Instruction Type Code	ROMPrgm[19..17]
Destination Register Code	ROMPrgm[16..14]
Operation Code	ROMPrgm[13..8]
Source Register Code	ROMPrgm[7..5]

2. All instructions use the ALU. An obvious design approach would be to use the ALU only for instructions that involved arithmetic or logical operations; i.e., RIO and RRO types. An alternative that simplifies the CPU design is to use the ALU for all instructions. In this case, an operator code (OPC[5..0]) and two operands (OP0[7..0] and OP1[7..0]) are assigned to every instruction type, then the ALU result is used or ignored as appropriate. Using this approach, all instructions have a commonality that simplifies overall circuit design.

Below are the operation codes and operands for each instruction type.

MVI – 000 ddd xxxxxx vvvvvvvv - Move immediate data value v..v to destination register ddd:

63

OPC[5..0] = "000000" addition without carry
OP0[7..0] = 0
OP1[7..0] = v..v

The ALU computes the sum of zero and immediate value v..v. The ALU result (immediate value v..v) is stored in the destination register ddd.

RIO – 001 ddd cccccc vvvvvvvv – Register-immediate operation:

OPC[5..0] = operation code cccccc
OP0[7..0] = destination register ddd value
OP1[7..0] = v..v

The ALU performs operation cccccc using the destination register ddd value and immediate value v..v as operands. The ALU result is stored in destination register ddd.

MOV – 010 ddd xxxxxx sss xxxxx – Move source register sss value to destination register ddd:

OPC[5..0] = "000000", addition without carry
OP0[7..0] = 0
OP1[7..0] = source register sss value

The ALU computes the sum of zero and source register sss value. The ALU result (source register sss value) is stored in the destination register ddd.

LDI - 011 ddd c x xxxx xxxx xxxx – Load destination register ddd indirectly from the Data ROM (DROM) if c = "0" or from Register Memory (MRAM) if c = "1". In either case, register pair DE contains the address.

OPC[5..0] = "000000", addition without carry
OP0[7..0] = 0
OP1[7..0] = Data byte at address HL in the Data ROM

The ALU computes the sum of zero and the specified value in DROM or MRAM. The ALU result (the specified value in DROM or MRAM) is stored in the destination register ddd.

RRO – 100 ddd cccccc sss xxxxx – Register-to-register operation:

OPC[5..0]= operation code cccccc
OP0[7..0]= destination register ddd value
OP1[7..0]= source register ss value

The ALU performs designated operation cccccc using the destination register ddd value and source register ss value. The ALU result is stored in the destination register ddd.

BRC -101 vvvv xxxx v vvvv vvvv – Branch conditional:

OPC[5..0]= "00000", addition without carry with result destination register "xxx" (don't care).
OP0[7..0]=0
OP1[7..0]=0

For the BRC type, dummy values of 0 are sent to the ALU then the ALU result is ignored[vii].

CRT -110 u vvvv vvvv vvvv vvvv – Call/Return unconditional:

OPC[5..0]= "00000", addition without carry with result destination register "xxx" (don't care).
OP0[7..0]=0
OP1[7..0]=0

For the CRT type, dummy values of 0 are sent to the ALU then the ALU result is ignored.

JIA -110 u vvvv vvvv vvvv vvvv – Jump/Replace instruction address with HL unconditional:

OPC[5..0]= "00000", addition without carry with result destination register "xxx" (don't care).

OP0[7..0]=0
OP1[7..0]=0

For the JIA type, dummy values of 0 are sent to the ALU then the ALU result is ignored.

3. Rising edge (positive logic) options will be used for all device inputs and outputs. This provides a consistency in the design that makes it less confusing.

4. While inputs may appear on more than one unit, outputs are unique appearing on only one unit. This is standard system design that again leads to less confusion and easier understanding of the computer's operation. It also simplifies the explanation of each unit's design. For each unit, we assume a set of inputs exist then design the circuitry to produce the unit's outputs. If, in the end, all inputs match outputs across all units without duplication of outputs, the circuit design is complete. This is the approach I used to create the design below.

Clock Unit Design

The Clock Unit (CU) generates clock pulses that initiate and coordinate execution of computer instructions. A typical instruction cycle consists of these steps:

(1) **Fetch** - Fetch an instruction from Program ROM
(2) **Decode -** Decode the instruction to see what is to be done
(3) **Execute** - Execute the instruction
(4) **Store -** Store the result.

These steps are not instantaneous. Truth table models may be, but real logic devices require a small but finite time to generate an output during each step. Thus, wait times must be built into the design. By applying appropriately timed clocking pulses to sequential devices, instructional steps can be carried out in proper order and time allowed for each to complete. Clock pulses within an instruction cycle are called *subclocks* and denoted them by T0, T1, ... Tn where n is the number of the subclocks needed for a given instruction. As we will see, n varies with different instructions.

In the BYOC CPU design, all instructions except PUSH complete in two subclocks. PUSH requires three. To accommodate this and speed up processing, the clock design generates three subclocks with a reset feature that restarts the clock after two subclocks for all but the PUSH instruction.

Subclocks are generated from an external clock. The figure below shows the relation between the external clock and subclocks for the case when n is 2.

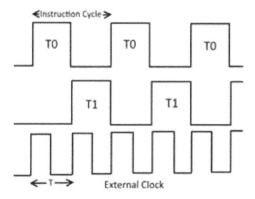

The duration of each subclock is one external clock cycle or T seconds. By adjusting the frequency of the external clock, both the number of instructions per second and duration T of each subclock is controlled.

Sequential devices are clocked on the rising or falling edge. Based on design constraint 3, the Logisim BYOC CPU design uses rising edges only allowing the remainder of the subclock on-time for the instructional step to complete. A typical instruction cycle breaks down this way:

    1. The instruction is fetched on the rising edge of subclock T0
    2. The instruction is decoded and executed during the remainder of T0
    3. The result is stored on the rising edge of T1 and has the remainder

of T1 to complete

4. A new instruction appears with next T0 rising edge and the instruction cycle repeats

As indicated earlier, the Clock Unit generates three subclock pulses, T0, T1, and T2. For convenience interconnecting units, these three signals are combined into a 3-bit bus SClk[2..0] where bit SClk[0] is T0, bit SClk[1] is T1, and bit SClk[2] is T2. At each unit, SClk[2..0] is split into the component subclocks T0, T1, and T2. The Clock Unit also supplies high active signal SRst that resets other units preparing them to execute the first instruction at address 0x0000 in ROMPrgm[19..0].

CU Inputs and Outputs

Inputs:

RUN – External signal to manually control execution (manual RUN/STOP)

RESET – External signal to manually reset CPU (manual RESET)

RClk – Restart clock signal that resets clock to T0 (SClk[2..0]="001")

Outputs:

SRst - System Reset signal activated by manual reset

SClk[2..0] - Subclocks bus where T0 is SClk[0], T1 is SClk[1], and SClk[2] is T2

CU Logisim Subcircuit Symbol

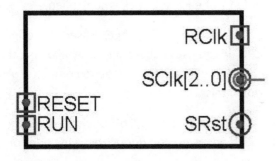

Note: Logisim inputs symbols are squares and outputs are circles.

CU Outputs

SRst – As shown below, output SRst connects directly to the RESET input. A manual RESET issues a SRst signal to all units putting them in a start-up state. SRst prepares the PCU to execute the instruction at the beginning of the Program ROM, (ROMAdrs[15..0] = 0x0000) and resets registers in the MU and ALU to a zero.

SClk[2..0] - To generate subclock output SClk[2..0], three D-type flip flops are configured as illustrated in the circuit below.

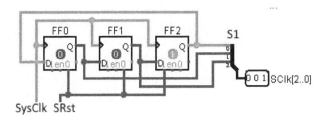

The Q output of each flip flop connects to the next D input. The third Q output connects back to the first D input. Input SRst connects to the asynchronous set/reset inputs of the flip flops so that a manual RESET places the first two flip flop outputs at "0" and the third flip flop output at "1". This is the CPU's initial state corresponding to subclock T0 or SClk[2..0] = "001".

SysClk connects to the clock inputs of all three flip flops, so that with each clock cycle, the "1" output rotates to the next flip flop. This generates the repeating sequence "001", "100", "010", "001" etc. in the outputs. Splitter S1 combines flip flop outputs in the proper order to create SClk[2..0]; i.e., so that SClk[0] is T0, SClk[1] is T1, and SClk[2] is T2.

Complete CU Circuit

Clock Unit

The addition of gates G1 and G2 completes the design. AND gate G1 between System Clock and the flip flop's clock inputs blocks the System Clock unless RUN is manually set to "1". OR gate G2 permits a flip flop reset pulse to reach the flip flops from either manual Reset or logic signal RClk. In either case, SClk[2..0] is set to "001", subclock T0. For all but the PUSH instruction, RClk resets the clock on the rising edge of T2 generating only subclocks T0 and T1. For the PUSH instruction, no RClk pulse is received allowing the clock to generate the full sequence T0, T1, and T2.

Note that a RESET starts the Clock Unit with T0 high. By doing so, the first instruction in the Program ROM passes through the fetch, decode, and execute steps then halts until RUN is raised to "1". At that point, System Clock pulses reach the flip flops; T0 ends; T1 starts the store step; and program execution is underway.

Program Control Unit

The Program Control Unit (PCU) manages the Program ROM including the Instruction Address Register that supplies the address of the instruction to be executed. The PCU also generates the operation code OPC[5..0] used by the ALU during the execution step of the instruction cycle.

70

PCU Inputs and Outputs Inputs:

Inputs
> **SRst** - System reset signal
> **SClk[2..0]** – Subclock bus
> **Zero** - Zero status signal indicating a zero ALU result
> **Carry** – Carry status signal indicating a carry ALU result.
> **HL[15..0]** – Combined H and L register pair bus for indirect

addressing (IAHL instruction)
> Outputs:
> > **ROMAdrs[15..0]** - Instruction word address bus
> > **ROMPrgm[19..0]** - Instruction word program bus
> > **OPC[5..0]** – ALU operation code bus

PCU Logisim Subcircuit Symbol

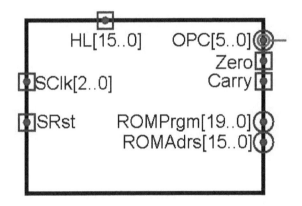

PCU Internal Signals and Buses

1. SRst – System reset signal connects to input SRst.

2. T0, T1, and T2 – Splitter S0 expands bus SClk[2..0] into subclock signals T0, T1, and T2.

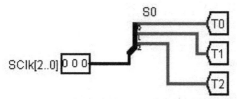

3. Various Signals – The circuit below contains several decoding subcircuits producing the internal signals described below. Splitter S9 expands the instruction word (ROMPrgm[19..0]) into its component bits from which the other signals are derived using a variety of decoding techniques.

ROMPrgm[19..0]

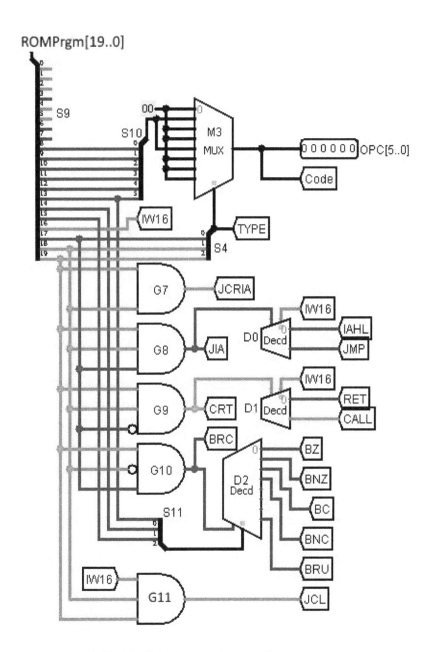

IW16 –IW16 is bit 16 of the instruction word.
TYPE[2..0] - Splitter S4 combines ROMPrgm[19..17] into bus TYPE[2..0],

the instruction type.

JCIA - Signal JCIA indicates a CRT or JIA instruction type. AND gate G7 decodes signal JCIA when ROMPrgm[19..18] is "11". The sum of products technique was used to design this circuit and many others that follow.

JIA - Signal JIA indicates a JMP or IAHL instruction. AND gate G8 decodes signal JIA when ROMPrgm[19..17] is "111".

IAHL and JMP – Signal IW16 (ROMPrgm[16]) distinguishes between IAHL and JMP instructions when signal JIA is "1". JIA connects to decoder D0's enable input. IW16 connects to D0's select input. When JIA is "1", D0 is enabled and generates signals IAHL when IW16 is "0" and JMP when IW16 is "1". The enable input of devices like this decoder is often used to select groups of codes. In this case, a code group (IAHL and JMP) is preselected by JIA then the specific instruction (IAHL or JMP) is further selected by IW16. Unless enabled by JIA, the decoder Do's output is "0" deselecting all.

CRT - Signal CRT indicates a CALL or RET instruction. AND gate G9 decodes CRT when ROMPrgm[19..17] is "110".

RET and CALL - IW16 (ROMPrgm[16]) distinguishes between RET and CALL instructions when CRT is "1". CRT connects to decoder D1's enable input. IW16 connects to D1's select input. When CRT is "1", D1 is enabled and generates signals RET when IW16 is "0" and CALL when IW16 is "1".

BRC - Signal BRC indicates a branch instruction. AND gate G10 decodes BRC when ROMPrgm[19..17] is "101".

BZ, BNZ, BC, BNC, and BRU – Decoder D2 generates these branching signals. Splitter S11 combines ROMPrgm[15..13] to drive the select input of D2. BRC connects to decoder D2's enable input. When BRC is "1", D2 is enabled and generates these signals:

Instruction	ROMPrgm[15..13]
BZ	000
BNZ	001
BC	010
BNC	011
Undef	100
Undef	101
Undef	110
BR	111

JCL - Signal JCL indicates JMP or CALL instruction. AND gate G11 decodes JCL when ROMPrgm[19..18] is "11" and IW16 is "1".

4. ZC - ZC indicates the current instruction is a branch and its associated condition is true. The truth table below summarizes the relationships between the Zero and Carry status bits and the branching conditions.

Inputs							Output
Zero	Carry	BZ	BNZ	BC	BNC	BR	ZC
1	X	1	0	0	0	0	1
0	X	0	1	0	0	0	1
X	1	0	0	1	0	0	1
X	0	0	0	0	1	0	1
X	X	0	0	0	0	1	1

Note: X="don't care".

Zero rows are not shown and ignored.

Applying the sum of products technique to the truth table produces the circuit below.

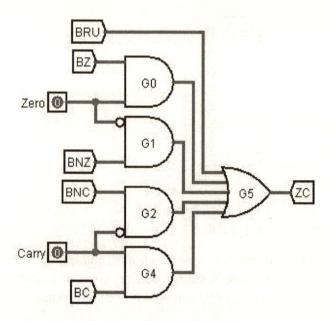

5. BVAL[15..0] and JCVAL[15..0] - Splitters S6 and S8 expand the instruction word ROMData[19..0] into its component bits 0 to 19.

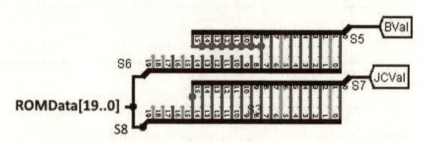

BVAL - BVAL[15..0] is the signed value added to the instruction address when branching occurs. Splitter S5 combines ROMPrgm[8..0] into bus BVAL{8..0}. ROMPrgm[8] is the sign bit and connects to bits 8 to 15 of BVAL filling out the 16-bit value. This has the effect of limiting the 16-bit value of BVAL to a signed numeric range of -256 to +255.

JCVAL - JCVAL[15..0] is the target address for unconditional JMP and CALL instructions. Splitter S7 combines ROMPrgm[15..0] into bus JCVAL[15..0].

PCU Outputs

1. ROMAdrs[15..0] - The circuit below generates the executing address ROMAdrs[15..0].

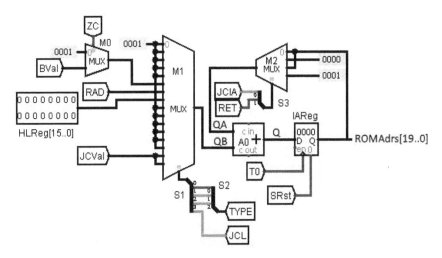

16-bit Adder A0's output Q is the sum of QA and QB. Q is the data input to Instruction Address Register IAReg that updates to the address of the next instruction ROMAdrs[15..0] on the rising edge of T0. The table below summarizes the expected values of QA, QB, and Q.

Signals					A0 Inputs		A0 Output
ZC	TYPE	JCL	JCIA	RET	QA	QB	Q = QA + QB = ROMAdrs[15..0]
0	BRC	0	0	0	Current address	1	Current address + 1
1	BRC	0	1	0	Current address	BVal[15..0]	Current address + BVal[15..0]
X	CRT	0	1	1	1	RAD[15..0]	RAD[15..0] + 1
X	CRT	1	1	0	0	JCVAL[15..0]	JCVAL[15..0]
X	JIA	0	1	0	0	HLReg[15..0]	HLReg[15..0]
X	JIA	1	1	0	0	JCVAL[15..0]	JCVAL[15..0]

Notes: For all other types, Q = Current Address + 1.
X="don't care"

JCL indicates a JMP or CALL instruction
RAD is the return address from a CALL

Multiplexers M1 and M2 generate QB and QA, respectively. The truth tables below were derived by splitting the truth table above. The first defines the selections for M1 and the second for M2.

Input	M1 Selects				M1 Inputs					Output
ZC	S3 JCL	S2 TYPE[2]	S1 TYPE[1]	S0 TYPE[0]	5	6	7	14	15	QB
0	0	1	0	1	1					1
1	0	1	0	1	BVAL					BVAL
X	0	1	1	0		RAD				RAD
X	1	1	1	0			JCVAL			JCVAL
X	0	1	1	1				HLReg		HLREG
X	1	1	1	1					JCVAL	JCVAL

Notes: For all other combinations, QB is 1.

M2 Selects		M2 Input				M2 Output
S1 JCIA	S0 RET	0	1	2	3	QA
0	0	Current Address				Current address
0	1		0			0
1	0			Current Address		Current Address
1	1				1	1

Instruction Address Register IAReg holds ROMAdrs[15..0] during the current instruction cycle. On the rising edge of T0, IAReg updates with the new , computed ROMAdrs[15..0]. System reset SRst connects to IAReg's asynchronous zero input resetting the starting address 0x0000 after a manual RESET.

2. ROMPrgm[19..0] - The Logisim ROM below is the Program ROM (PROM) for the CPU. PROM output D is the instruction word ROMPrgm[19..0] located at address ROMAdrs[15..0]. The Program ROM is a Logisim 64,536-byte, 8-bit wide ROM.

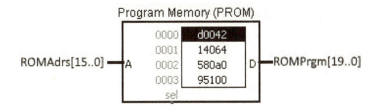

Program Memory (PROM)

ROMAdrs[15..0] ──► A | 0000 | d0042 | D ──ROMPrgm[19..0]
0001	14064
0002	580a0
0003	95100
sel	

3. OPC[5..0] - Operation code OPC[5..0] is "000000"(add without carry) for all instruction types except RRO (type "100") and RIO (type "001"). For these, OPC[5..0] comes directly from the ALU code in instruction word. See the circuit below.

ROMPrgm[19..0]

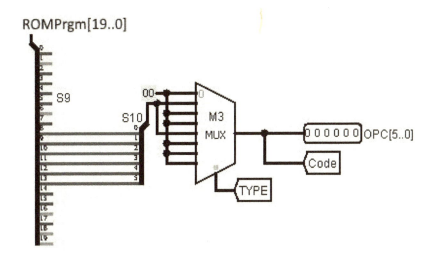

Splitter S9 expands ROMPrgm[19..0] to individual bits 0 to 16. Splitter S10 combines ROMPrgm[13..8], the instruction word ALU operation code, to produce the RRO and RIO options (1 and 4 respectively) for multiplexer M3. The remaining options for other types are "000000". M3's select input is connected to instruction type bus TYPE[2..0].

Additional PCU Circuits - Call/Return

The call/return and push/pop circuitry were the most difficult to design and troubleshoot. They utilize an adder to calculate the address where data is to be stored. Beyond that, the design required considerable experimentation to get right. Timing plays a critical role in the workings of both including requiring an additional subclock T2.

Call/return instructions provide a way to make programs more compact and understandable. The same code appearing multiple times in a program can be replaced by a CALL to a single copy of the code (called a subroutine). A RET instruction in the subroutine returns execution to the instruction following the associated CALL. The call/return circuit below creates a last-in-first-out (LIFO) stack to store the return address RAD. With the 256-byte Logisim 16-bit wide RAM, up to 256 levels of calls are permitted.

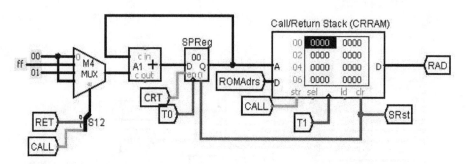

Adder A1 calculates the stack address for CRRAM. One A1 input is the current stack address. Multiplexer M4 supplies the other by selecting 1 (0x01) for a CALL instruction or -1 (0xFF) for a RET instruction. The result is that the stack address increments on a CALL and decrements on a RET. On a CALL, T1 clocks CRRAM and stores the address of the CALL instruction. On a RET, the stored address plus 1 becomes the new executing address. (See output Item 1 above, ROMAdrs[15..0], for the associated RET circuitry.) With this, execution returns to the instruction following the associated CALL.

Below is the complete PCU circuit.

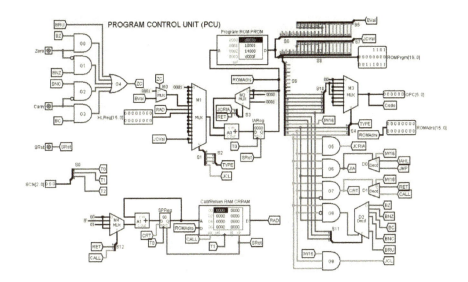

Memory Unit

The Memory Unit (MU) manages the CPU's general purpose registers, the Memory RAM (MRAM), the Push/Pull Stack (PPRAM), and the Data ROM (DROM). It generates operands OP0[7..0] and OP1[7..0] used by the ALU, handles external inputs and outputs, and produces the reset clock signal RClk. The MU also provides register outputs for CPU monitoring and interfacing with other units.

MU Inputs and Outputs

Inputs:

SRst - System reset signal

SClk[2..0] – Subclock bus

ROMPrgm[19..0] - Instruction word

ALUR[7..0] - ALU operation result

IOINP[7..0] - External I/O data input

Outputs:

B[7..0], C[7..0], D[7..0], E[7..0], H[7..0], L[7..0], M[7..0] and A[7..0] – General purpose register buses

81

OP0[7..0] and OP1[7..0] – ALU operand code bus

HL[15..0] – Combined H and L register pair bus for indirect addressing (IAHL instruction)

IOOUT[7..0] – External I/O data output bus

IOR and IOW – Read and write clocking signals for external devices

IOPort[7..0] – External I/O port number bus

RClk – Restart clock signal

MU Logisim Subcircuit Symbol

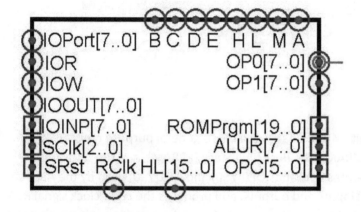

MU Internal Signal and Values

1. SRst – System reset signal connected to input SRst.

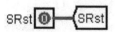

2. T0, T1, and T2 – Splitter S6 expands bus SClk[2..0] into subclock signals T0, T1, and T2.

82

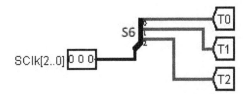

3. LRAM, RIO, and RRO – Splitter S3 expands the instruction word (ROMPrgm[19..0]) into its component bits from which the other signals are derived.

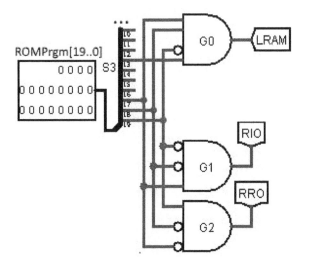

> **LRAM** – Signal LRAM indicates a LRAM instruction. AND gate G0 decodes signal LRAM when ROMPrgm[19..17] combined with ROMPrgm[13] is "0111".
>
> **RIO and RRO** – Signals RIO and RRO indicate RIO and RRO instruction types, respectively. AND gate G1 decodes signal RIO when ROMPrgm[19..17] is "001". AND gate G2 decodes signal RRO when ROMPrgm[19..17] is "100".

4. Various Signals – Splitter S4 expands the instruction word (ROMPrgm[19..0]) into its component bits from which the other signals are derived. The circuits below contain several decoding subcircuits that are active only for instruction types RIO and/or RRO.

83

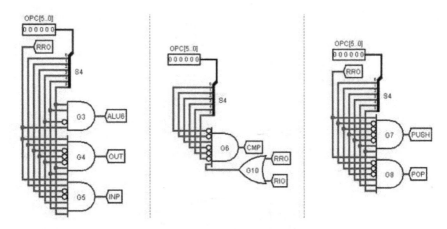

ALU9 – ALU6 indicates a Level 6 ALU instruction (such as PUSH and OUT). These instructions require special treatment because they do not store the ALU result in a destination register. For PUSH, the destination is the PUSH/POP Stack. For OUT, it an external I/O device. AND gate G3 decodes an ALU Level 6 instruction when OPC[5..3] combined with RRO is "1101".

OUT and INP – Signals OUT and INP indicate OUT and INP instructions, respectively. AND gate G4 decodes signal OUT when OPC[5..0] combined with RRO is "1100011". AND gate G5 decodes signal INP when OPC[5..0] combined with RRO is "1110011".

CMP – Signal CMP indicates a CMP or CPI instruction. AND gate G6 decodes signal CMP when OPC[5..0] and either RRO and RIO (via OR gate G10) is "0001001".

PUSH and POP – Signals PUSH and POP indicate PUSH and IPOP instructions, respectively. AND gate G7 decodes signal PUSH when OPC[5..0] combined with RRO is "1100001". AND gate G8 decodes signal POP when OPC[5..0] combined with RRO is "1110001".

5. DestReg[7..0] and SrceReg[7..0] – These buses provide the values of the destination and source registers as coded in the instruction word. In the circuit below, multiplexers M3 and M4 use buses

84

Dest[2..0] and Srce[2..0] to select the destination register value DestReg[7..0] and the source register value SrceReg[7..0] for the current instruction, respectively.

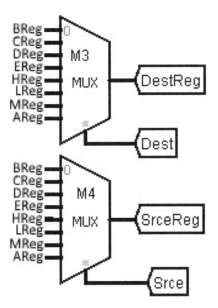

6. PVAL[7..0] and IVAL[7..0] Values; Srce[2..0], Dest[2..0], and TYPE[2..0] Signals - Splitter S3 expands the instruction word (ROMPrgm[19..0]) into its component bits from which these signals are derived.

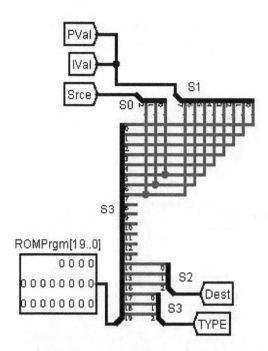

PVAL[7..0] and IVAL[7..0] – Bus PVAL[7..0] is the I/O port number used by external I/O instructions. IVAL[7..0] is the immediate value used by RIO type instructions. Splitter S1 combines ROMPrgm[7..0] into buses PVAL[7..0] and IVAL[7..0].

Srce[2..0] - Bus Srce[2..0] is the source register as specified in the instruction word. Splitter S0 combines ROMPrgm[7..5] into Srce[2..0].

Dest[2..0] - Bus Dest[2..0] is the source register as specified in the instruction word. Splitter S2 combines ROMPrgm[16..14] into Dest2..0].

TYPE[2..0] - Bus TYPE[2..0] is the instruction type as specified in the instruction word. Splitter S3 combines ROMPrgm[19..17] into TYPE[2..0].

MU Outputs

1. AReg[7..0], BReg[7..0], CReg[7..0}], … MReg[7..0] - The circuit below includes general purpose registers B, C, D, E, H, L, A, and memory register M.

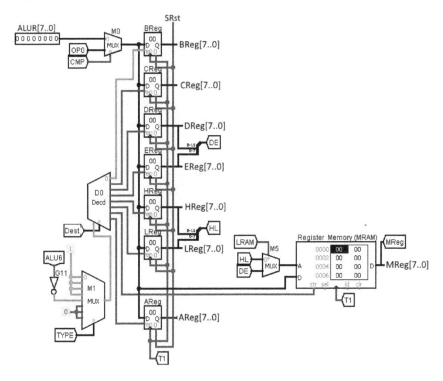

It consists of seven 8-bit registers and a 65,536 byte 8-bit RAM. Decoder D0's outputs connect to register and memory enable inputs so that the destination code Dest[2..0] connected to its select input enables the device to be updated on the rising edge of T1. General purpose registers including the memory register do not update for all instruction types. To account for this, D0's enable input is connected to multiplexer M1's output. In turn, M1's select input connects to TYPE[2..0]. Its data inputs 0 to 3 connect to "1" enabling D0 and allowing updates for types MVI, RIO, MOV, and LDI. A "0" on inputs 5 to 7 inhibits updating for types BRC, CRT, and JIA.

M1's data input 4 , representing type RRO, is a special case. All ALU operation codes except Level 6 update a destination register. As previously noted, Level 6 instructions have destinations other than registers. An inverted ALU6 signal connects to M1's data 4 input providing the correct logic (a "0" for Level 6) to inhibit updates for Level 6 operations.

Data input for the registers and MRAM is the ALU result ALUR[7..0] except for compare instructions (CMP and CPI). For these, multiplexer M0 selects operand OP0[7..0], the destination register value. Thus, for CMP and CPI instructions, the destination register is updated to its own value (left unchanged) while the Zero and Carry status registers update as usual. For example, CMP A,B subtracts B from A setting Zero and Carry status, but unlike the SUB instruction, A is left unchanged. System reset SRst connects to the asynchronous reset inputs of the registers (not MRAM) zeroing them when a manual RESET occurs.

2. OP0[7..0] and OP1[7..0] - The circuit below generates ALU operands OP0[7..0] and OP1[7..0].

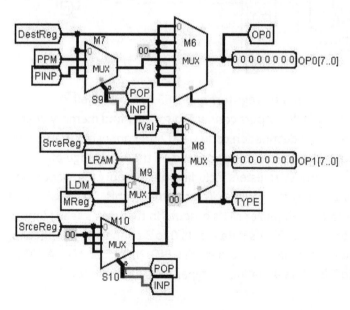

Operands differ by instruction type. The select inputs of multiplexers M6 and M8 connect to bus TYPE[2..0]. Their data inputs differ by instruction type as described below.

MVI – Move Value Immediate (IVAL OP0[7..0] is zero. OP1[7..0] is IVAL.

RIO – Register-to-Immediate Operation OP0[7..0] is the destination register to be operated on. OP1[7..0 is IVAL.

MOV – Move source register to destination register.

OP0[7..0] is zero.

OP1[7..0] is source register.

LDI – Load Destination Register Indirectly from DROM or MRAM. OP0[7..0] is zero. OP1[7..0] is DROM output (LDM[7..0]) or MRAM output (MReg[7..0]). Multiplexer M9 selects LDM[7..0] or MReg[7..0] based on signal LRAM.

RRO – Register-to-Register Operation OP0[7..0] is destination register, top of push/pop memory stack (PPM[7..0]) or external I/O input (PINP[7..0]). Multiplexer M7 selects PPM[7..0] or PINP[7..0] based on signals POP and INP or destination register otherwise. OP1[7..0] is source register or zero. Multiplexer M7 selects aero on signals POP and INP or source register otherwise.

BRC – Branch conditional OP0[7..0] is zero. OP1[7..0] is zero.

CRT – Call/Return OP0[7..0] is zero. OP1[7..0] is zero.

JIA – Unconditional jump or replace instruction address OP0[7..0] is zero. OP1[7..0] is zero.

3. HL[15..0] - The circuit below supplies HL[15..0] to the PCU for the IAHL instruction.

4. IOPort[7..0], IOOut[7..0], IOR, and IOW - The circuit below generates external I/O outputs.

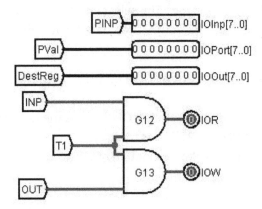

IOINP[7..0] is the source for internal signal PINP[7..0] providing a path for external I/O data to a register or DRAM via the memory register. IOPort[7..0] connects to bus PVAL[7..0] providing the port number for the external I/O devices. IOOut[7..0] connects to DestReg[7..0] supplying data from a register to an external I/O device . AND gates G12 and G13 are gated by T1 to produce I/O control signals IOR (I/O Read) and IOW (I/O Write). In a later chapter, I describe how to configure external I/O devices using these signals.

5. RClk - The circuit below generates the RClk output.

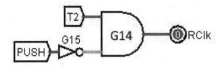

All instructions except PUSH require only subclocks T0 and T1. To handle this, signal RClk resets the Clock Unit on the rising edge of T2 except for PUSH when AND gate G14 blocks T2 allowing the Clock Unit to generate T1, T2, and T3.

6. Additional MU Circuits - The MU contains two additional circuits. The first is the Data ROM (DROM) below.

90

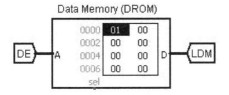

It consists of a 65,536 byte 8-bit wide ROM with its address driven by register pair DE. ROM output is bus LDM[7..0].

The second circuit is the PUSH/POP Stack Memory below.

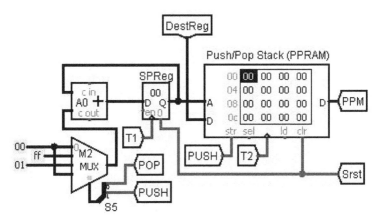

The design is identical to the CALL/RETURN circuit described in the PCU section. The difference is the destination register value DestReg[7..0] is pushed on to the stack to be later popped off as bus PPM[7..0]. PPRAM is a 256-byte 8-bit wide RAM which means that up to 256 values can be pushed on to the PUSH/POP Stack.

This is the complete Memory Unit circuit.

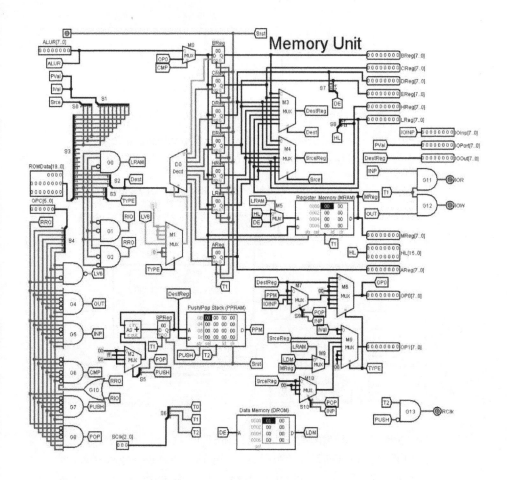

Arithmetic Logic Unit

The Arithmetic Logic Unit (ALU) performs a variety of arithmetic and logical operations using an ALU operator code OPC[5..0] and two ALU operands, OP0[7..0] and OP1[7..0]. ALU result ALUR[7..0] is returned to the MU for storage as indicated by the instruction. In addition, the ALU generates signals Carry and Zero used for branching by the PCU.

ALU Inputs and Outputs
Inputs

SRst - System Reset

SClk[2..0] – Subclock bus

ROMPrgm[19..0] - Instruction Word

OPC[5..0] - ALU operator code

OP0[7..0] and OP1[7..0] - ALU Operands

Outputs:

ALUR[7..0] - ALU Result bus

Carry and Zero Status signals

ALU Logisim Subcircuit Symbol

ALU Internal Signals and Values

1. SRst – System reset signal connected to input SRst.

2. T0, T1, and T2 – Splitter S0 expands bus SClk[2..0] into subclock signals T0, T1, and T2.

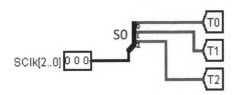

3. Level[2..0], Code[2..0], and ARTH – The circuit below generates these signals.

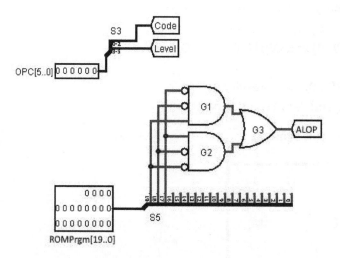

Level[2..0] and Code[2..0] – The ALU operations are divided into eight groups or levels and within each level are eight operations or codes. Levels have related characteristics based primarily on the way they affect the Zero and Carry signals. Levels are designated ALU0[7..0], ALU1[7..0],..., ALU7[7..0]. For instance, Level 0 contains all the arithmetic operations with ALU0[7..0] the operational result. Splitter S3 expands the operation code OPC[5..0] into two buses: OPC[5..3] as Level[2..0] and OPC[2..0] as Code[2..0].

ALOP – Signal ALOP (Arithmetic/Logic Operation) indicates an instruction type RRO and RIO. Splitter S5 expands ROMPrgm[19..0] into 19 bits. AND gate G1 decodes RRO when ROMPrgm[19..17] is "100". AND gate G2 decodes RIO when ROMPrgm[19..17] is "100". OR gate G3 combines signals RRO and RIO to produce the signal ALOP.

ALU Outputs

94

1. ALUR[7..0] – ALUR{7..0] is the result of ALU operation OPC[5..0] and operands OP0[7..0] and OP1[7..0]. The circuit below shows that multiplexer M0's select input connects to bus Level[2..0] and its data inputs connect to the eight Level results, ALU0[7..0] to ALU7[7..0].

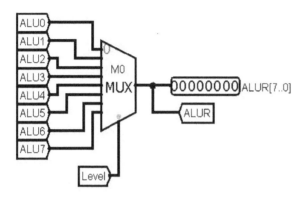

Individual Level results are described below.

Level 0 Basic arithmetic operations

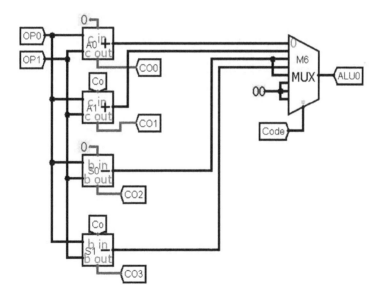

Multiplexer M6 uses Code[2..0] to select one of the operations described below. OP0[7..0] contains the value of the destination register. OP1[7..0] contains the immediate value for RIO operations or the value of the source register for RRO operations.

Code "000" – Adder A0 adds OP0[7..0] and OP1[7..0] with carry-out CO0.
Code "001" – Adder A0 adds OP0[7..0] and OP1[7..0] plus carry-in CO with carry-out CO1.
Code "010" – Subtractor S0 subtracts OP1[7..0] from OP0[7..0] with carry-out (borrow) CO2.
Code "011" – Subtractor S1 subtracts OP1[7..0] from OP0[7..0] less carry-in CO with carry-out (borrow) CO3.
Code "100" – Subtractor subtracts OP1[7..0] from OP0[7..0] with carry-out (borrow) CO2. This is a compare instruction (CMP or CPI), so this ALU0[7..0] and ALUR[7..0] are ignored.
Codes "101", "110", and "111" - Unused.

Level 1 Unused (Available for future expansion)

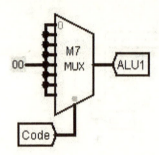

Level 2 Increment/decrement registers

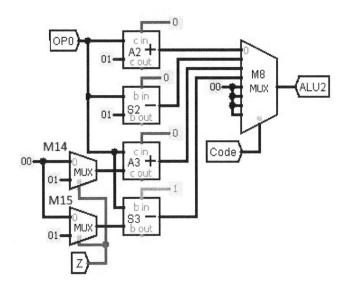

Multiplexer M8 uses CODE[2..0] to select one of the operations described below. OP0[7..0] contains the value of the register to be incremented.

Code "000" – Adder A2 adds 1 to OP0[7..0].

Code "001" – Subtractor S2 subtracts 1 from OP0[7..0].

Code "010" – Using multiplexer M14, adder A3 adds 0 to OP0[7..0] if signal Z is "0" or 1 if Z is "1".

Code "011" – Using multiplexer M15, subtractor S3 subtracts 0 from OP0[7..0] if signal Z is "0" or 1 if Z is "1".

Codes "100", "101", "110", and "111" - Unused.

Level 3 Basic logic operations

97

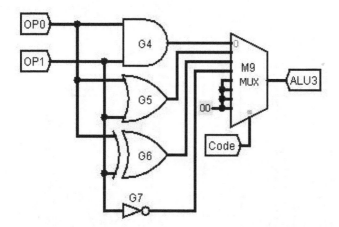

Multiplexer M9 uses CODE[2..0] to select one of the operations described below. OP0[7..0] contains the value of the destination register. OP1[7..0] contains the immediate value for RIO operations or the value of the source register for RRO operations.

Code "000" – AND gate G4 performs bit-wise and operation on OP0[7..0] and OP1[7..0].

Code "001" – OR gate G5 performs bit-wise or operation on OP0[7..0] and OP1[7..0].

Code "010" – XOR gate G6 performs bit-wise exclusive-or operation on OP0[7..0] and OP1[7..0].

Code "011" – Inverter G7 "inverts OP1[7..0].

Codes "100", "101", "110", and "111" - Unused.

Level 4 Rotate registers

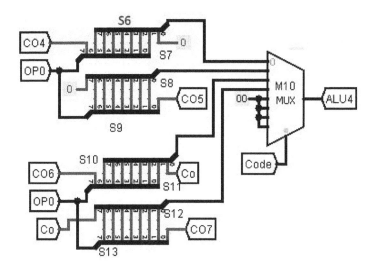

Multiplexer M10 uses CODE[2..0] to select one of the operations described below. OP0[7..0] contains the value of the register to be rotated.

Code "000" – Splitters S6 and S7 are arranged to offset bits of OP0[7..0] one position to the left. "0" is assigned to bit position 0 and bit position 7 is assigned to carry CO4.

Code "001" – Splitters S8 and S9 are arranged to offset bits of OP0[7..0] one position to the right. "0" is assigned to bit position 7 and bit position 0 is assigned to carry CO5.

Code "010" – Splitters S10 and S11 are arranged to offset bits of OP0[7..0] one position to the left. CO is assigned to bit position 0 and bit position 7 is assigned to carry CO6.

Code "011" – Splitters S12 and S13 are arranged to offset bits of OP0[7..0] one position to the right. CO is assigned to bit position 7 and bit position 0 is assigned to carry CO7.

Codes "100", "101", "110", and "111" - Unused.

Level 5 Unused

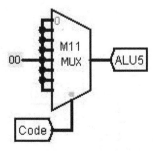

Level 6 PUSH and OUT instructions

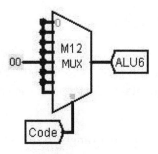

For Level 6, the destination is something other than a register. For the PUSH instruction, the destination register value is stored on top of the Push/Pop stack. For the OUT instruction it is passed via IOOut to the external I/O output device. The result ALU6[7..0] is returned with a zero value and ignored.

Level 7 POP and INP instructions

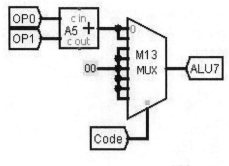

Using Code[2..0], multiplexer M13 selects the output of adder A5 for codes "000" (POP) and "001" (INP). For other codes, the selection is zero. The values OP0[7..0] and OP1[7..0] to be summed are more complicated in Level 7 because the source is not a register and varies depending on the instruction. Multiplexers M7 and M9 in the MU select the values for OP0[7..0] as described in the table below.

Code[2..0]	Instr	OP0[7..0]	OP1[7..0]
"000"	POP	PPM – Top of P/P Stack	0
"001"	INP	IOINP – Value of ext I/O value	0
"010" – "111" Unused			

2. Carry - Carry is the output of the Carry Register CReg and indicates that a carry resulted from a previous arithmetic operation. Logic operations reset (zero) the Carry Register. The Carry circuit is shown below.

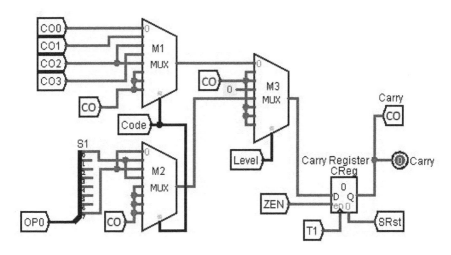

Level[2..0] connects to the select input of multiplexer M3. As inputs to M3, multiplexers M1 and M2 further refine the choice of what value supplies data for Carry Register CReg. Possible options are as follows:

Arithmetic operations

101

Code "000" - CO0, the carry out of adder A0 (ADD and ADI instructions)

Code "001" – CO1, the carry out of adder A1 (ADC and ACI instructions)

Code "010" – CO2, the carry-out of subtractor S0 (SUB and SUI instructions)

Code "011" – CO3, the carry-out of subtractor S1 (SBB and SBI instructions)

Code "100" – CO2, the carry-out of subtractor S0 (CMP and CPI instructions)

Codes "101", "110", and "111" – CO (the current value of CReg) leaving Carry unchanged

Increment/decrement registers - CO (the current value of CReg) leaving Carry unchanged

Basic logic operations reset Carry – "0"

Rotate registers

> **Code "000"** – OP0[7]
> **Code "001"** – OP0[0]
> **Code "010"** – OP0[7]
> **Code "011"** – OP0[0]
> **Codes "100", "101", "110", and "111"** – CO (the current value of CReg) leaving Carry unchanged

PUSH and OUT - CO (the current value of CReg) leaving Carry unchanged

POP and INP - CO (the current value of CReg) leaving Carry unchanged

M3's output is connected to the data input of the CReg. Connecting signal ALOP to CReg's enable input restricts updating to RIO and RRO instruction types only. As with all register updating, the rising edge of

T1 clocks and updates CReg. Lastly, SRst connects to CReg's asynchronous zero input resetting it after a manual RESET.

3. **Zero** - Zero is the output of the Zero register ZReg and indicates that a zero resulted from a previous arithmetic operation. The Zero circuit is shown below.

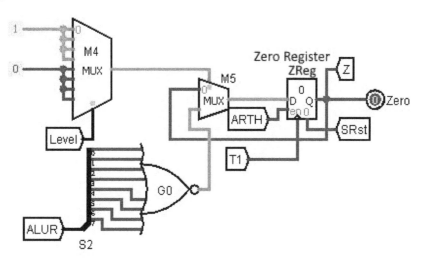

NOR gate G0 output is "1" only when an ALU operational result is zero. Multiplexer M4's select inputs are arranged so that ALU Levels 0 to 3 produce a "1" output and Levels 4 to 7, a "0" output. M4's output drives the select input of multiplexer M5 controlling whether the Zero Register updates with G0's output (Levels 0 to 3) or its own output leaving the value of Zero unchanged (Levels 4 to 7). Signal ARTH connects to the enable input of ZReg so that the Zero Register only updates for arithmetic instructions. ZReg updates on the rising edge of T1 and zeros on manual RESET (SRst).

The figure below shows the complete Arithmetic Logic Unit.

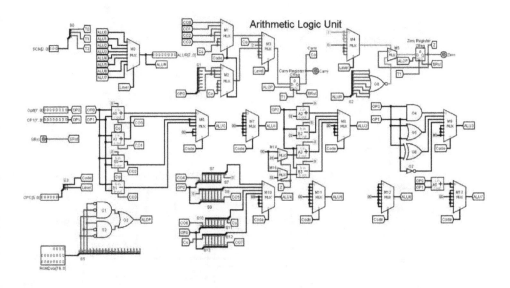

Complete BYOC CPU

The figure below shows the complete CPU with units interconnected. Units outputs (red dots) connect to their respective inputs (blue dots). As suggested by Constraint 4, (1) Outputs are unique while inputs are not, (2) Every input is supplied by an output within the circuit, and (3) Every output is generated within a single unit from the its inputs. This being true we have system completeness for the design. Logisim hex output displays were added to monitor the program as it executes. Simple binary outputs were included to monitor registers. External inputs RUN and RESET connect to binary inputs for CPU control. Poking RESET to "1" and back to "0" resets the CPU. Poking RUN to "1" starts execution.

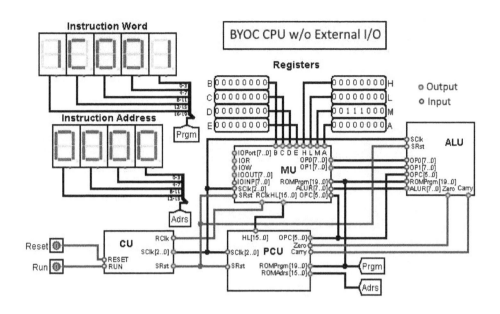

Chapter 7 – Testing the BYOC CPU

Testing Strategy

The testing strategy used was to begin with very simple programs that exercised specific instructions like MOV and ADD. Then proceed to test instructions of all eight types, building more and more complex programs that exercised instruction in various combination. Finally came programs that more fully utilized the CPU's capabilities and provided some assurance that the CPU was relatively bug free.

The Instruction Cycle

Before proceeding, let's review the steps in the instruction cycle:

Step 1. At the rising edge of subclock T0, the PCU fetches the instruction ROMPrgm[19..0] (the output of PROM) at ROMAdrs[15..0] (the output of register IAReg).

Step 2. PCU logic develops the ALU operator code OPC[5..0] and MU logic develops the two ALU operands OP0[7..0] and OP1[7..0].

Step 3. ALU logic uses the ALU operator code OPC[5..0] and the ALU operands OP0[7..0] and OP1[7..0] to generate the result ALUR[7..0]. The remainder of T0 provides time for the combinational logic in steps 1 to 3 to establish a stable result.

Step 4. On the rising edge of subclock T1, (a) sequential logic in the ALU captures the Zero in ZReg, the Carry result in CReg, and (b) sequential logic in the MU captures the ALU result ALUR[7..0] in its general purpose registers.

Step 5. During the remainder of T1, the ALU and MU memory devices complete storage of ALU results. Also, PCU combinational logic develops the next address to execute in adder PCU A0.

Step 6. Return to Step 1 with the next address ready to be captured in IAReg on the rising edge of T0.

Branch, call, and jump instructions follow the same steps except that Steps 2 to 4 are ignored.

Logisim Troubleshooting

Logisim provides several troubleshooting features:

1. Stop and Step - Use Logisim's control code Ctrl K and Ctrl T to stop and step through an instruction cycle. Ctrl K toggles the Logisim clock off and on. Toggling Crtl T multiple times issues successive subclocks T0 and T1. For example,

Step 1. Toggle Crtl K to turn off the Logisim clock.

Step 2. Hover over a unit in the main view, right-click the mouse, and left click the "View" option to see the state of all wires and components in the unit. This is a "live" view as opposed to the "edit" view. Logic values change as subclocks are triggered.

Step 3. Toggle Crtl T to step through subclock cycles and check to see the program instructions execute as expected.

2. Poke a Wire or Bus – Use the Poke tool to poke a wire or bus and show its logic value. A pop up will show a "0" or "1" for a wire and the binary/decimal value for a bus.

3. Continuous Monitoring - Connect the Probe tool to a wire or bus to continuously monitor logic values.

4. Simulate test conditions - By using the Poke tool to set logic values on inputs, test conditions can be simulated. For example, to check combinational logic associated with an instruction, set the unit's ROMPrgm[19..0] input to an instruction and check for expected logic values. For sequential logic, poke SClk[2..0] bit positions to simulate subclocks then check that logic actions occur in the correct sequence.

Initial Testing

The count-down example program introduced in Chapter 5 is a good first test for the CPU.

Address	Instruction	Hex	ASM Code	Description
0	000 111 000000 00000001	1C001	START: MVI A,1	Move 1 to A. A=1
1	010 010 000000 111 00000	480E0	MOV D,A	Move A to D. D=1 and A=1.
2	000 111 000000 00000101	1C005	MVI A,5	Move count 5 to A. A=5.
3	100 111 000010 010 00000	0C240	LOOP: SUB A,D	Subtract D=1 from A and store in A.
4	101 0 001 0000 111111111	A21FF	BNZ LOOP	Branch on not zero back 1 to LOOP and subtract D=1 again. When A=0, fall through to line 5.
5	111 1 0000 0000 0000 0000	F0000	JMP START	Jump to START and do over

The new "Hex" column was added to accommodate the data entry requirement of the Logisim HEX editor. The steps to download the program into the Program ROM (PROM) are shown in the figure below.

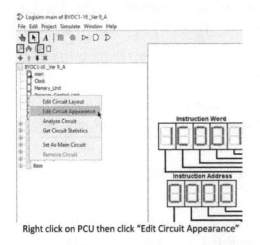

Right click on PCU then click "Edit Circuit Appearance"

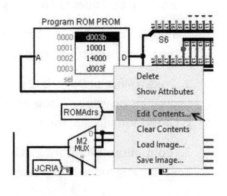

Right click on PROM and select "Edit Contents"

For testing, a slower Logisim clock rate than the maximum 4.1 KHz is advisable. To change the rate, click on "Simulate—Tick Frequency" and select 32 Hz or even slower if warranted. After following the first three steps below, the program executes automatically as shown in the frames below.

Frame 1. With RUN "0", poke RESET to "1" and back to "0".

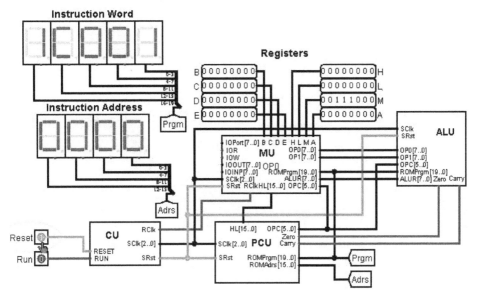

Frame 2. Poke RUN to "1". First instruction MVI A,1 executes. A is now 1.

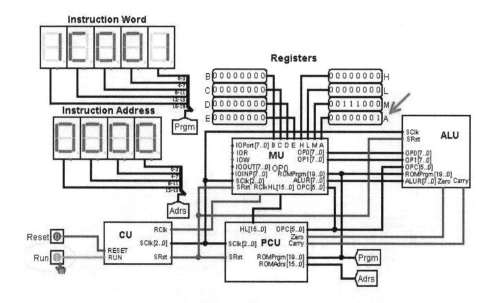

Frame 3. MOV D,A executes. Both D and A are now 1.

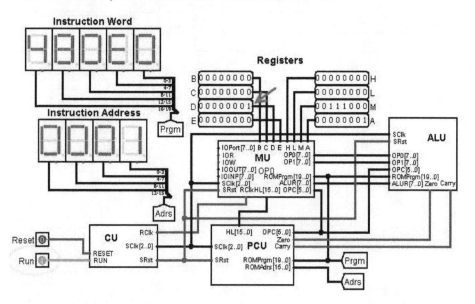

Frame 4. MVI A,5 executes. A is now 5 ("101").

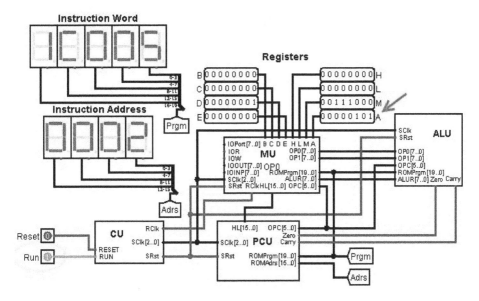

Frame 5. SUB A,D executes. A is now 4.

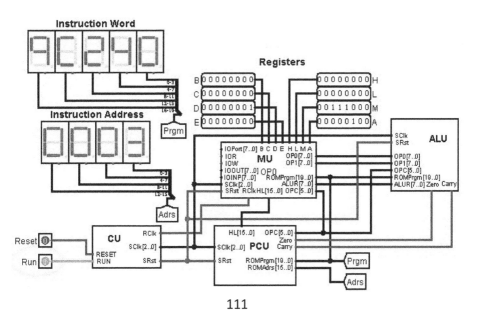

Frame 6. Since the subtraction did not yield zero (Zero status dark green "0"), BNZ LOOP branches back 1.

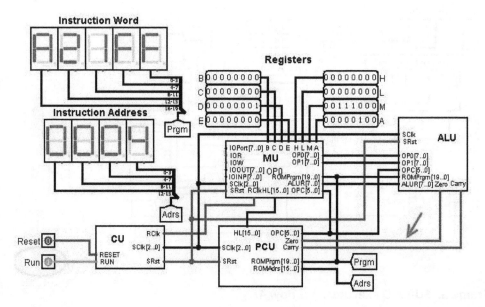

Frame 7. SUB A,D executes again. This sequence repeats until A is 0.

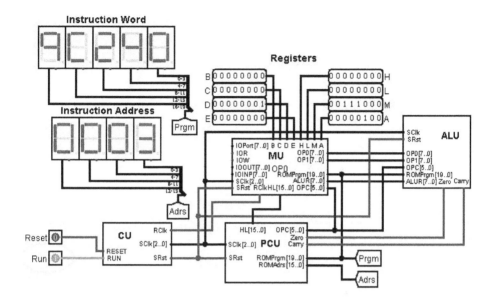

Frame 8. When A is 0, executions fall through BNZ LOOP to JMP START (0x0000) and the program starts over.

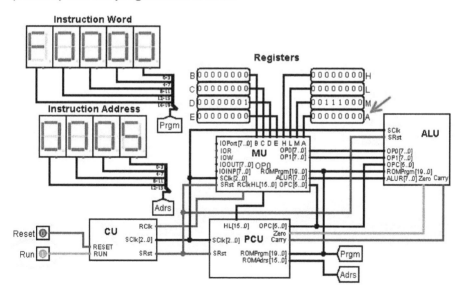

Advanced Testing

This simple counting program shows the instruction cycle is functioning properly and verifies instruction types MVI, MOV, RRO, BRC, and JIA are executing correctly. To test the RIO type, the variant of the program introduces the logic operation ANI A,255 to detect when register D zero counts.

start:	mvi	d,5
loop:	dcr	d
	ani	d,255
	bnz	loop
	jmp	start

A further test program below checks CRT type instructions with two levels of CALL and RET instructions.

start:	mvi	a,15
	call	sub0
self:	jmp	self
sub0:	mov	d,a
	call	sub1
	ret	
sub1:	mvi	a,10
	ret	

After execution, A is 10 and D is 15.

The final instruction type LDI is tested with this program.

```
start:                 mvi          h,0
                       mvi          l,4
                       mvi          m,5
                       mvi          d,0
                       mvi          e,4
                       lram         a
                       lrom         b
self:                  jmp          self
```

It checks that the memory register M is working, and that data can be read from the Data ROM. Address 4 in DROM is edited to load withaddress 4 with 15. After execution, A is 5 and B is 15.

A crucial test to check PUSH/POP instructions is shown below.

```
start:                 mvi          a,15
                       mvi          d,10
                       push         a
                       push         d
                       pop          a
                       pop          d
loop:                  jmp          loop
```

Several other test programs were created to verify instructions and combinations of instructions. Testing the BYOC CPU helped identify several circuit errors that were corrected. While I cannot say that tests were exhaustive, I gained enough confidence to try more complex programs.

The Sieve of Eratosthenes algorithm finds prime numbers from 1 to a specified number n. A prime number is a number divisible only by itself and one. Examples are 2, 3, 5, 7, 11, 13, ... The algorithm is described below.

Step 1. Make list of the numbers from 1 to n.

Step 2. Start with number 2 and strike out (make zero) all multiples of 2.

Step 3. Move upward to the next unstruck (non-zero) number, in this case 3, and repeat the strikeout of multiples.

Step 4. Continue until the square root of n is reached.

Step 5. The numbers left unstruck (non-zero) are primes.

Beginning with the SIEVE100 program below, an assembler created in Excel was used to generate program code.

Step 1 fills the first 100 locations in DRAM.

```
;
;  Sieve of Eratosthenes – SIEVE100
;
;    Generate Primes on range 1 to 100
;
;    Fill the first 100 locations of RAM with values 1 to 100.
;
start:      mvi         l,100               ;HL is the pointer to DRAM
            mvi         h,0
            mvi         e,100               ;E is max value
loop0:      mov         m,e                 ;Store  value
            dcr         l                   ;Decrement address
            dcr         e                   ;Decrement value
            bnz         loop0               ;If value not zero, do again
```

Steps 2 and 3 strike multiples:

```
;
;   Zero all multiple locations up to Square Root(100) = 10
;
            mvi         c,2                 ;Start with 2 as base value
loop1:      mov         l,c                 ;Set DRAM pointer to address of base value
            or          m,m                 ;Has the base value been stricken?
            bz          next_n              ;If so, move on to next value to strike
loop2:      add         l,c                 ;Otherwise, compute address of multiple
            mvi         m,0                 ;Zero location to strike
            cpi         l,101               ;Have multiples 100 or less been  stricken?
            bc          loop2               ;If not, strike another
next_n:     inr         c                   ;Otherwise, next base value
            cpi         c,10                ;Reached 10?
            bnz         loop1               ;If not, do multiple zeroing again
self:       jmp         self                ;Otherwise, done
```

See Appendix A for a detailed description of the BYOC Assembler. The program listing is annotated using the semicolon. All text to the right of the semicolon is a comment ignored by the assembler.

After executing the program, the only way to display the results was to view the contents of MRAM. While viewing the MU, right-clicked on MRAM, and select "Edit Contents". This is the result.

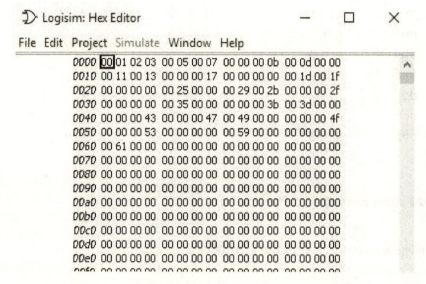

The non-zero values displayed here in hex are the expected primes!

Viewing memory values is an inefficient way to communicate with a computer. In the next the next chapter, I add a display and keyboard to the BYOC CPU.

Chapter 8 – External Input/Output

External I/O Basics

To make computers useful, they must communicate effectively with the outside world. Besides communicating with humans, computers also are used to acquire external data and control external devices. To accomplish this, circuits are needed that connect or interface the CPU to external I/O (Input/Output) devices.

In this chapter, three interfacing units are described. The first interfaces the computer to a keyboard and display. The second is an interface that supports external on/off devices like LEDs and switches. The third provides a method of acquiring a random number for use in game programming. In each case, an I/O unit is described that contains the circuitry required for each case.

To handle multiple, external I/O devices, each is assigned a port number from 0 to 255. The BYOC CPU INP and OUT instructions can then reference the port number when communicating with the device. For instance, the instruction INP B,4 addresses the device assigned to port 4 and inputs an 8-bit data value on that port to the B register. For OUT 1,A, the contents of register A outputs an 8-bit data value to the device assigned to port 1.

Sometimes, external I/O devices require a control port in addition to a data port. For a simple keyboard device, the control port provides a status bit that indicates that a key has been pressed and a character is ready for inputting. The data port is then accessed to retrieve the character.

In the case of a display device, a "busy" status bit on the control port indicates that it is not ready to receive another character. It should be noted that there are other, far more efficient ways to control input and outputting, but they require a more advanced CPU design.

Terminal Unit

The BYOC Terminal Unit (TU) design is shown below.

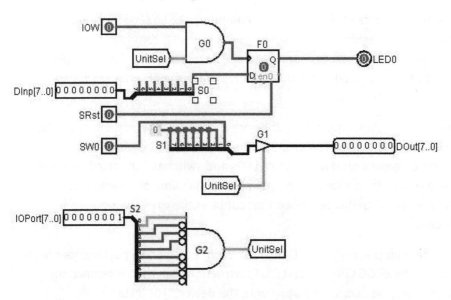

The control port (port 4) is input only and has two status bits: a "1" on bit 7 indicates when the display is busy and a "1" on bit 6 indicates that a keyboard character is available for input. The Logisim display (the TTY) has no busy signal, so bit 7 connects to "0" indicating it is never busy. The data port (port 5) handles input from the keyboard and output to the display.

AND gate G2 decodes the unit port number 4. When IOPort[7..1] equals "0000010", signal UnitSel (Unit Select) is "1" indicating the Terminal Unit is selected. The remaining bit, IOPort[0], functions as signal PortSel. It is "0" for control port 4 or "1" for data port 5. AND gates G0 and G1 use UnitSel and PortSel gated with IOR and IOW to generate the display clock DspClk and keyboard clock KbyClk signals. DspClk clocks Logisim TTY to display the character on DspOut[7..0]. KbyClk places the keyboard's next available character on KbyInp[6..0].

Multiplexer M0 is enabled only when the unit is selected (UnitSel is "1"). In that case, if PortSel is "0", M0 output is the control byte consisting of TTY busy on bit 7 and keyboard data available on bit 6. Again, the TTY has no busy signal, so bit 7 is connected to "0". If PortSel is "1", M0 output is the available keyboard character from KbyInp[6..0].

Note that the keyboard ASCII character consists of only bits 0 to 6. This is why KbyInp[7] is connected to "0" to complete TUOut[7..0]. It is also why splitter S2 picks off only the lower six bits of S1 (TUInp[7..0]) to make DspOut[6..0]. Refer to the internet for complete listings of the 7-bit ASCII codes for characters, numbers, and symbols.

M0's is configured so that when M0 is not selected (enable is "0") , its output is "floating". This allows multiple devices to share the IOInp[7..0] bus. Below is the Logisim subcircuit symbol for the Terminal Unit and the CPU with it installed.

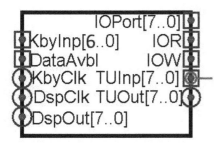

The code below echoes a keyboard character on the TTY display.

```
;
;  Echo Program
;
Start:          call        bin
                call        bout
                jmp         start
;
;  Input Character to B from Keyboard
;
bin:            inp         b,4             ;Is a character available?
                ani         b,0b01000000    ;Check bit 6, character available
                bz          bin             ;If not, try again
                inp         b,5             ;Otherwise, get the character
                ret                         ;Return to the calling routine
;
;  Output Single Character in B
;
bout:           inp         b,4             ;Is TTY busy?
                ani         b,0b10000000    ;Check bit 7, display busy
                bnz         bout            ;If so, wait
                out         5,b             ;Otherwise, display character
                ret                         ;Return to calling routine
```

Note: To use the Logisim keyboard, move the cursor inside the keyboard symbol and left click. The character typed will show only an instant then reappear on the display.

The figure below shows execution after typing "Hello World".

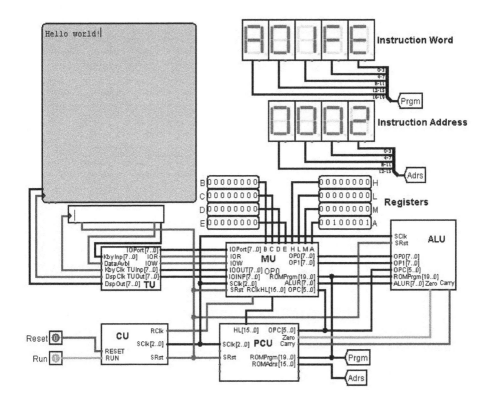

Digital Unit

The Digital Unit interfaces the BYOC CPU to simple on/off devices like LEDs and switches. In this case, no control port is required. The data port is 1 and has both input and output capabilities. See the circuit below.

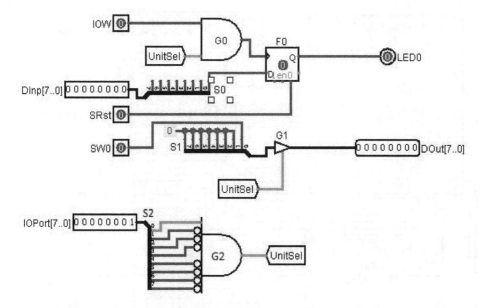

AND gate G2 decodes the UnitSel when IOPort[7..0] is 1. The single digital input SW0 connects via splitter S1 to controlled buffer G1. When the unit is selected (UnitSel = "1"), SW0's value (either "0" or "1") is placed on bit 0 of DOut[7..0] and inputted to the CPU. On the data output side, bit 0 of the referenced register connects to the data input of D-type flip flop F0 via splitter S1. When the unit is selected (UnitSel = "1") and the I/O write signal IOW arrives, F0 is clocked and the register value is loaded into F0 and output to LED0.

This is the Logisim subcircuit symbol for the Digital Unit.

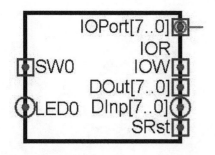

124

The code below tests the Digital Unit.

```
start:   inp  a,1   ; Input switch status to A
         out  1,a   ;Output switch status to LED

         jmp  start ;Repeat
```

Toggling input SW0 toggles the LED. See below.

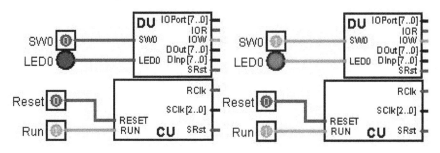

Random Number Unit

When programming games, generating a random number is often needed. A simple way to accomplish this is to randomly sample the count of an 8-bit counter connected the fast changing clock signal (SysClk in this case). The counter continuously counts from 0 to 255 and rolls back to 0. When a player presses the keyboard at some random time, the value in the counter at that moment is input to a register. Modulo 100 code operates on the value to reduce it to a random value from 0 to 100.

To make a counter, simply connect D-type flip flops as shown below.

125

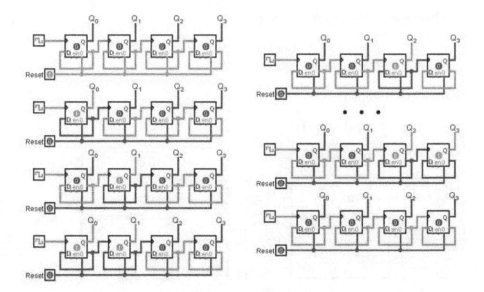

The inverted output of each flip flop connects back to its D input and to the clock input of the next flip flop. Connecting the inverted output to the D input results in the flip flop changing output states with each clock pulse. In the first frame above, all the flip flops are zeroed. In subsequent frames, clock pulses to the first flip flop propagate through the other flip flops. The result is that outputs Q3 to Q0 sequence through binary values "0000", "0001", "0010", "0011", so forth to "1111" and finally back to "0000". The 0 to 15 count can be extended 0 to 255 by adding four more flip flops.

The 8-bit Logisim counter C0 is the heart of the Random Number Unit design shown below.

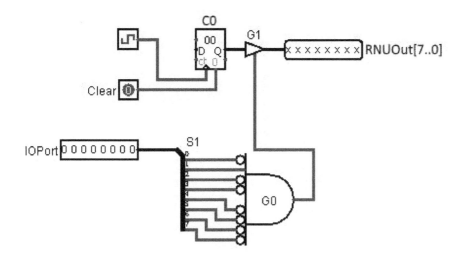

Port number 2 is the data port for the RNU. It is implemented with the decoding circuit AND gate G0. The system clock connects to the 8-bit counter C0 causing it count continuously. Controlled buffer G1 places the counter value on the RNUOut output whenever the instruction INP r,2 is executed. The 8-bit value read at that instant is transferred to register r becoming the value used in a program. Note that G1's output is "floating" when not enabled.

The code below shows a typical use of the RNU.

```
;
; Get Random Number 0 to 100 in E
;
get_rnd_num:       call        new_line          ;New line
                   mvi         h,0               ;Point HL to 'Press any key..." message
                   mvi         l,msg8
                   call        mout              ;Display message
get_rnd_num_0:     inp         a,cntr_port       ;Get keyboard control byte
                   ani         a,64              ;Is character available?
                   bz          get_rnd_num_0     ;If not, keep checking
                   inp         a,data_port       ;Otherwise, clear keyboard data port
                   inp         e,rnd_port        ;Get random value into E
get_rnd_num_1:     sui         e,101             ;Compute modulo 100
                   bnc         get_rnd_num_1
                   adi         e,101
                   ret                           ;Return to calling routine
```

When the user presses a key, the value that happens to be in the counter transfers to the E register. Modulo code adjusts the value to a range less than 100.

Below is the Logisim symbol for the RNU.

Complete BYOC CPU with External I/O

The BYOC CPU with added external I/O units is below.

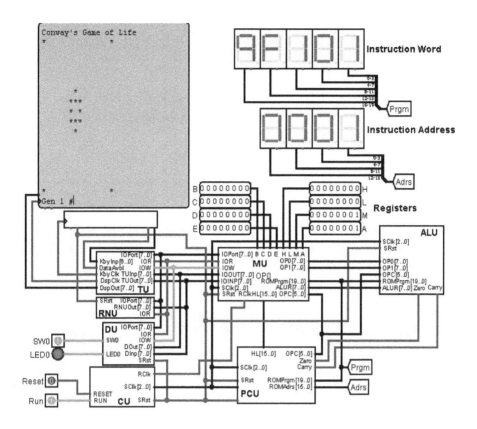

In the next chapter, I develop programs using the I/O units and put the BYOC CPU through its paces.

Chapter 9 – Programming the BYOC CPU

With the addition of external I/O capability, I put the BYOC CPU through its paces with programs that demonstrate more of its capabilities.

Sieve of Eratosthenes – SIEVE100-1

The SIEVE100-1 program below adds the display capability of the CPU to the original SIEVE 100 program and shows prime numbers in decimal format. The subroutine DOUT makes the binary to printable ASCII conversion. A second subroutine MOUT tests access to the Data ROM (DROM) by displaying an ASCII character string stored in DROM. The annotated listing of expanded SIEVE100 program is found in Appendix D.

Executing the SIEVE100 program produces this result.

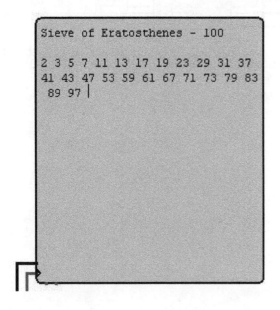

```
Sieve of Eratosthenes - 100

2 3 5 7 11 13 17 19 23 29 31 37
41 43 47 53 59 61 67 71 73 79 83
 89 97 |
```

High/Low Number Guessing Game

The next program uses keyboard data entry. It is a number guessing program sometimes called High/Low. This is a basic outline of the program steps.

Step 1. Display program title.

Step 2. Display instructions

Step 3. Get a random number from 1 to 100 hidden from player.

Step 4. Get guess from player and count tries.

Step 5. Display whether guess was high, low, or equal.

Step 6. If equal, display "Got it" message and number of tries.

Step 7. If high or low, state as such, and get another guess (go to step 4).

Step 8. Go back for another game (go to step 2).

See Appendix E for a complete listing. The figure below shows a typical game played with the program.

```
BYOC Number Guess Game

I am thinking of a number
between 1 and 100.
Press any key to continue
Your guess? 50
Too high.  Try again.
Your guess? 25
Too low.  Try again.
Your guess? 33
Too low.  Try again.
Your guess? 35
You got it in 4 tries.

I am thinking of a number
between 1 and 100.
Press any key to continue
```

Conway's Game of Life

The third test program tested is an implementation of Conway's Game of Life. It is based on a 16 by 16 matrix of cells where live cells are indicted by an asterisk. Initially, a pattern of live cells is placed in the matrix. For each generation of life, the following rules are applied:

1. Any live cell with fewer than two live neighbors dies, as if by underpopulation.

2. Any live cell with two or three live neighbors lives on to the next generation.

3. Any live cell with more than three live neighbors dies, as if by overpopulation.

4. Any dead cell with exactly three live neighbors becomes a live cell, as if by reproduction.

The pattern changes with each generation producing interesting results.

Two 16x16 grids (grid 0 and grid 1) are created in MRAM. A starter grid of patterned 1s and 0s is copied into grid 0. Grid 0 is displayed and copied to grid 1. The cells in grid 0 are checked using the rules above and the values in grid 1. Grid 0 cells are updated according to the result and when all cells have been checked, the process is repeated using the newly updated grid 0.

Each cell is surrounded by eight neighbor cells to be checked. Given there are 16 x 16 or 256 cells in a grid, then each generation requires 8 X 256 = 2048 checks. Multiply this by the number of instructions required for each check and the number of executed instructions runs into the tens of thousands! Because of Logisim's relatively slow processing speed (4100 instructions per second), each generation takes nearly 3 minutes! Shown below are the four generations of a test cell pattern. See Appendix F for a complete listing.

```
Conway's Game of Life
*                      *




            *
           ***
           * *
           ***
            *




*              *
Gen 1 |
```

```
Conway's Game of Life
*                      *



           ***
           * *
          *   *
           * *
           ***



*              *
Gen 2 |
```

```
Conway's Game of Life
*                      *



            *
           * *
          ** **
          ** **
          ** **
           * *
            *


*              *
Gen 3 |
```

```
Conway's Game of Life
*                      *



            *
          ** **

         *     *

          ** **
            *


*              *
Gen 4 |
```

Note: The corners of the grid are marked with a permanent live cell. While the processing complexity of the Life program was a great confidence builder, it also showed the painfully slow execution speed of the simulator. The time had come to move on to a hardware implementation. In Chapter 10 I introduce Quartus and prepare to implement the BYOC CPU on the Intel Cyclone V FPGA.

Chapter 10 – Introducing the FPGA

FPGA Basics

As already noted, hand wiring the BYOC CPU can be avoided by utilizing programmable logic found in a Field Programmable Gate Array like the Intel Cyclone V. Coupled with Intel's Quartus design software, it is possible to make a hardware version of the BYOC CPU. Because I could not discover a way to directly import a Logisim design into Quartus, I had to enter the Logisim design as a Quartus schematic. Though time consuming, it provided a good introduction to Quartus. Once done, it remained only to compile, program, troubleshoot the FPGA. After a few weeks, I achieved the goal set at the outset to build a working computer.

Describing how to use Quartus is beyond the scope of this book. As with Logisim, the internet contains numerous helpful video tutorials showing how to get started with Quartus. Quartus Prime Lite can be download free from here[4]. An Intel introductory document that I found useful for getting in the beginning is found here[5].

The Cyclone V GX Starter Kit is good choice for the beginner as it is highly versatile and relatively inexpensive. The GX Starter Board includes the Intel Cyclone V GX (5CGXFC5C6F27C7N) FPGA and comes with an array of useful on-board resources for experimentation. It is available from Mouser Electronics and Digikey Electronics.

I used Quartus's block diagram/schematic mode to create the BYOC design. As with Logisim, Quartus supplies many basic components like primitive gates. See the Quartus Symbol Tool description in Appendix B. Unlike

---

[4] http://fpgasoftware.intel.com/?edition=lite

[5]

https://www.intel.com/content/dam/www/programmable/us/en/pdfs/literature/tt/tt_my_first_fpga.pdf

Logisim, more complex devices like multiplexers and decoders must be configured and saved in the project. These "megafunction" devices are found in an IP (Intellectual Property) Catalog and configured for specific requirements. See Appendix C for additional information on using the Quartus IP Catalog.

Compiling a design consists of several stages: (1) analysis and synthesis, (2) place and route, (3) assemble (generate programming files), (4) perform timing analysis, and (5) write netlist. If compilation is without errors, a pin planner associates inputs and outputs in the compiled design with components on the GX Starter Board. Among the latter are LEDs, switches, push buttons, a 4-digit hex display, external connectors such as for an Arduino, audio and HDMI interfaces, micro SD card, and 4 Mbyte SRAM.

After compiling and assigning pins, I used functional simulations to test the design. The "University Program VWF" simulation is good for beginners. Its use is described in any number of video tutorials. Bill Kleitz is a college instructor who has produced several helpful videos including the one found here[6] that covers how to use the University Program simulation tool. Most basic troubleshooting took place with this simulation tool. The last step was to use the built-in USB-Blaster to program the Cyclone V and do final hardware testing.

The Transition from Logisim to Quartus

Making the transition from Logisim to Quartus design was not without difficulties. Some were easy to overcome, and others took considerable research and time. The following general comments describe the difficulties I encountered and my approach to overcoming them.

1. No way was known to import the Logisim BYOC design. As already mentioned, the Logisim BYOC design had to be reentered using the Quartus Block Diagram/Schematic mode. Quartus' drag and drop schematic design

---

[6] https://www.youtube.com/watch?v=a8JAkKhxlQI

was very much like Logisim. Subcircuits could be made into block symbols so that the design could be done using the same operational units as with Logisim. See the figure below.

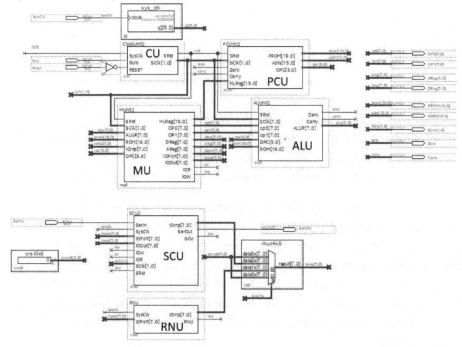

These differences are noted:

1. The more versatile SCU (Serial Communication Unit) replaced the Logisim TU (Terminal Unit). The SCU implements a more general serial interface that can be used with a standard keyboard/display terminal.

2. The DDU (Digital Display Unit) replaced the simpler Logisim DU to support the four seven-segment displays on the GX Starter Board.

3. The GX Starter Board's built-in clock operates at 50 MHz. To provide a slower speed for testing, a 26-bit counter C0 was added between the built-in clock and the BYOC CPU. By selecting specific bits of the counter's output, it is possible to change to speeds as low as 1 Hz.

4. The addition of multiplexer m0 to the CPU was necessary because I was not successful in implementing the Quartus floating output option for sharing outputs on the the IOInp[7..0] bus. The multiplexer is a work around.

2. Quartus does not have Logisim "tunnels". Wire and bus naming replaced tunnels in the Quartus design. For single wire connections, wires were named in their properties option. Here is an example from the Memory Unit.

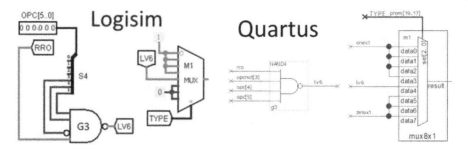

The left image shows the Logisim tunnel LV6 that connects G3's output to one of M1's inputs. The right image shows the Quartus implementation. The output wire from gate G3 is named "lv6" as is the input wire to multiplexer M1. When the Quartus circuit is compiled, wires of the same name are connected just as with tunnels.

Similarly, Quartus handles buses by naming the bus with bit designations. PPM[7..0] is a tunnel in Logisim's Memory Unit. In Quartus, the naming of bus as ppm[7..0] serves the same purpose as in the example of PUSH/PULL RAM and multiplexer M7 below.

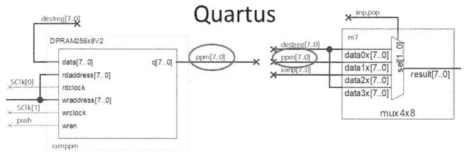

3. Quartus does not have Logisim splitters. Splitting and combining signal is done in Quartus using named wires and buses. See the example in the figure below.

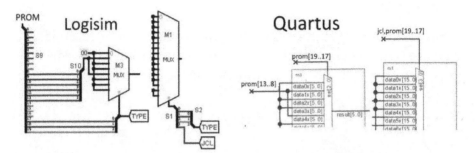

On the right, the wire jcl and bus prom[19..17] are combined by naming the select bus jcl,prom[19..17] where the components are separated by commas and the left-most component is most significant.

Also, on the left, Logisim splitter S9 expands the instruction word (PROM) into individual bits. The splitter S10 combines bits 13 to 8 into OPC[5..0] (the ALU operation code) for input to multiplexer M3. In the right figure, a Quartus bus wire named "prom[13..8]" accomplishes the same thing by specifying bits 13 to 8 of PROM. As another example, instruction type is bits 19 to 17 of PROM and is extracted in the Quartus design by using PROM{19..17] as the select input of M3. Combining JCL and TYPE[2..0] in the select input of multiplexer M1 is implemented in Logisim with splitters S1 and S2.

4. Quartus does not provide an option to invert inputs to primitive gates like AND and OR. Inverters were added as necessary.

5. Potential timing issues inherent in FPGA designs. Timing issues did not appear with Logisim, but it had to be considered with the FPGA design. The methods used to implement logic in FPGAs can introduce problematic time delays. Signals can arrive at critical points at different times resulting in logic errors.

To avoid timing issues, these strategies were followed in the BYOC Quartus design.

   A. Avoiding tandem logic – Strings of tandem logic were avoided, as they introduced unwanted delays. In the figure below, the left circuit with tandem multiplexers has the same truth table as the one on the right with only one multiplexer. The latter is preferred as it eliminates the tandem multiplexers and introduces less delay.

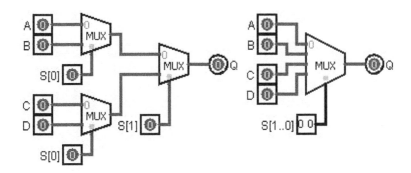

   B. Gated Clocks – In producing subclocks T0 and T1, it was necessary to gate the system clock. Gating clock is a known problem with FPGAs and must be avoided. The gating circuit used in the Clock Unit followed the recommendations in the Intel Handbook. Refer to the Intel document here for a full description.

   C. Clock resetting - Resetting the clock to change the number of subclocks proved to be problematic. Because of this, the Clock Unit was redesigned to make T0 and T1 non-overlapping as illustrated in the figure below.

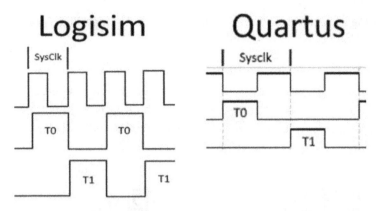

In the Logisim design, the falling and rising edges of T0 and T1 overlapped. This precluded using both rising and falling edges for timing. Therefore, the Logisim design used only rising edges. By separating T0 and T1 in the Quartus design, both rising and falling edges could be used for timing. Using all four edges satisfied all instruction timing and data settling requirements without the need for a third subclock.

To provide slower speeds for testing, the 50 MHz clock source clocking frequency was reduced with a 26-bit counter. By selecting bits of the counter output q[25..0], the BYOC's clock rate was controlled over a wide range. With q[n] connected to SysClk input of the Clock Unit, the processor speed is determined by the formula $50*106 / (2n+2)$. In the example below, n is 8 and the resulting processor speed is 48,828 instructions per second. This proved to be a good speed for most testing. The Sieve and Life programs have been successfully tested to n=0 or 12.5 million instructions per second! At that processor speed, Life runs at 68 generations per second or 12,400 times faster than the Logisim simulation!

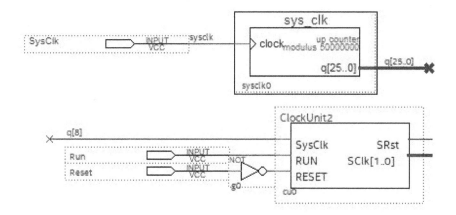

6. USB-Blaster driver conflicts with Serial Data USB. A software driver conflict arises when both the USB-Blaster USB for programming and the Serial Data USB or terminal communication are plugged in at the same time. No solution was found except plugging them in one at a time.

7. Program and data ROM initialization differ from Logisim. Programming Logisim ROMs was done with the Logisim HEX editor. Quartus relies on project files either in "hex" or "mif" format. I chose to use "mif" format and adapted the Excel assembler to produce a compatible listing that could be copied and pasted into a "mif" file. Shown below is the assembler output for the test program used previously.

Label	Instruction	Address	Object Code	MIF Code
START:	MVI A,1	00	1C001	**0 : 1C001;**
	MOV D,A	01	480E0	**1 : 480E0;**
	MVI A,5	02	1C005	**2 : 1C005;**
LOOP:	SUB A,D	03	9C240	**3 : 9C240;**
	BNZ LOOP	04	A21FF	**4 : A21FF;**
	JMP START	05	F0000	**5 : F0000;**

For Quartus, the "MIF Code" column (highlighted in bold) is copied and pasted into the MIF file as shown below. A good editor for this purpose is Notepad++ available from www.notepad-plus-plus.org.

143

-- Quartus Prime generated Memory Initialization File (.mif)
WIDTH=20;
DEPTH=4096;
ADDRESS_RADIX=UNS;
DATA_RADIX=HEX; CONTENT BEGIN

        0 : 1C001;
        1 : 480E0;
        2 : 1C005;
        3 : 9C240;
        4 : A21FF;
        5 : F0000;
[6..4095] : 00;
END;

The BYOC project file name for the program code is "BYOC-PROM.MIF". The data ROM is handled in a similar way. The file name in this case is "BYOC-DROM.MIF".

See Appendix A for additional insight into using the Excel BYOC assembler.

8. RAM memory exhibited read/write problems. Perhaps the most difficult problem encountered relates to RAM memory. Logisim RAM was not clocked or "registered" (Quartus terminology). As soon as an address appeared on Logisim RAM's address input, data appeared on its output. Quartus "megafunction" RAM did not work this way. Single-port Quartus RAM requires clocking the address during read/write operations resulting in RAM output changing at the wrong time during an instruction cycle.

The solution was to use dual-port RAM that had separate read and write clocking. By clocking read and write inputs at different times, the problem was solved. Shown below are the Logisim and Quartus versions of the Push/Pull Stack Memory.

Logisim RAM

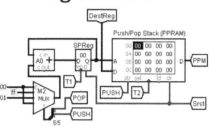

Quartus

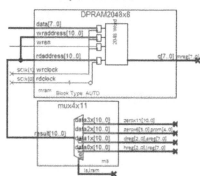

The Logisim RAM is clocked only on the rising edge of T2. The Quartus read address is clocked on the falling edge of T1 (inverted SClk[0][xi]) while the write address and RAM update are clock later, on the rising edge of T1 (SClk[1]).

Three I/O units were developed for the Quartus BYOC design . They are described in detail below.

Serial Communication Unit

The Serial Communication Unit (SCU) interfaces with a standard terminal (display and keyboard). The GX Starter Board version of the SCU is shown below.

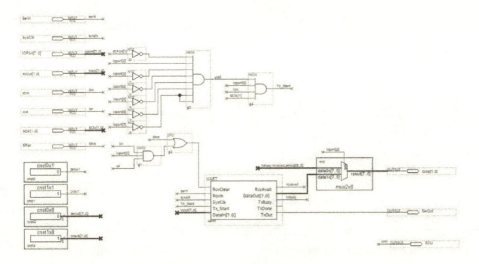

As with the Logisim design, the control and data ports are 4 and 5 respectively. AND gate g0 decodes the port unit as signal "usel". Gates g1 and g2 provide decoding for data port 5 inputting the character and clearing the receive buffer. AND gate g4 decodes output to data port 5 with signal "TX start" starting transmission of the character to be displayed.

A "megafunction" Universal Asynchronous Receiver Transmitter device (UART) provides serial conversion between parallel BYOC register data and the serial input/output ports. Multiplexer m0 selects the boards output to be either control data (RcvAvail or TxBusy) or keyboard data. Output SNU signals that the SCU Unit has been selected and is used to select the SCU output as input to the CPU ioinp[7..0] bus. See the "floating" drive discussion in General Comments item 1d.

To set the UART baud rate, follow these steps.

Step 1. In the Project Navigator, find UART.bdf and double click.

Step 2. Select the UART_TX, right click, and click "Parameters"

Step 3. Change to the "Parameter" tab.

Step 4. Double click "g_CLKS_PER_BIT Value" and enter 434.

Step 5. Click OK.

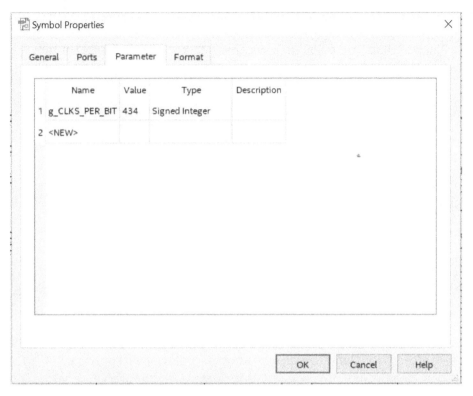

The number 434 is determined by dividing the system clock frequency 50*106 (50 MHz) by the desired baud rate 115,200.

Digital Display Unit

The Digital Display Unit (DDU) interfaces the BYOC with the GX Starter Board Hex Display. Rather than displaying hex digits, the DDU displays only digits 0 to 9. A BYOC register's lower four bits outputted to a selected digit displays "0000" to "1001" as a seven segment representation of decimal values 0 to 9. This coding scheme is called Binary Coded Decimal (BCD). The four digits, right to left, are associated with data ports 8 to 11. For example, if register

B's value is 6, "OUT 8,B" displays the number 6 on the rightmost hex digit. Output ports 9 to 11 display the remaining three hex digits. The DDU circuit is shown below. Four bits of digital input data are designed into the DDU. DInp0 to DInp3 are mapped to switches SW6 to SW9 on the GX Starter Board.

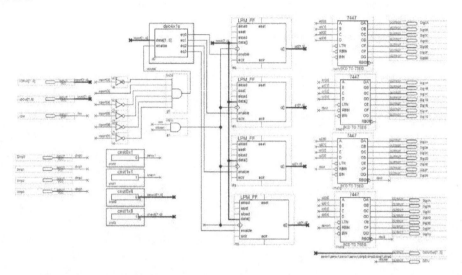

AND gate g0 and decoder d0 perform the port decoding of 8 through 11 selecting D-type flip flops ff0 through ff3 that hold the outputted value. AND gate G1 gates IOW with the DDU select signal (ddusel) to clock the flip flops.

Quartus contains a large inventory of IC chips, one of which is the 7447 that performs the BCD to seven segment conversion. The 7447 outputs are assigned to the GX Starter Board's four Hex Digit Displays. The four digital inputs are simply passed through to DDUOut[7..0] and ultimately to multiplexer m0 for routing to IOInp[7..0] when the an INP rd,8 instruction is executed. The upper 4 bits are zero. As designed, up to eight bits are accommodated.

Random Number Unit

The design of the Random Number Unit (RNU) is essentially the same as the Logisim and is given below.

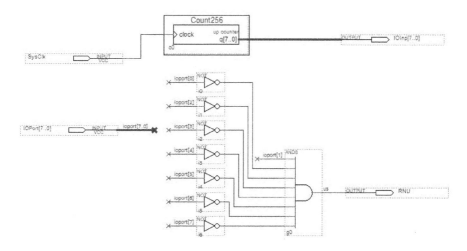

Signal RNU indicates that the RNU port 2 is selected.

Input Selection Workaround

As already noted, lack of a floating output capability means that data outputs of the SCU, RNU and DDU cannot connect to ioinp[7..0] at the same time. Multiplexer m0 below selects which one does. Signals SCU, RNU, and DDU provide the select input for m0.

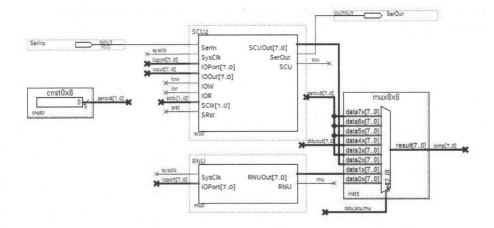

Pin Assignments

BYOC circuit inputs and outputs are assigned to components on the GX
Starter Board. See the figure and list below.

The GX Starter Board has ten slide switches and four push buttons. Reset is assigned to push button KEY3 and Run to slide switch SW0.

The eighteen GX Starter Board LEDs are assigned as follows: the left-most two to the subclock output (SClk[1..0]), the next eight to the A register and the right-most 8 to the D register. In testing, the A and D register LEDs are frequently used to display test results.

The Digital Display Unit (DDU) is connected to the GX Starter Board's 4-digit 7-sement hex display and switches SW9 to SW6.

The UART device in the Serial Communication Unit (SCU2) interfaces with the GX Starter Board External USB port. When used with a PC terminal emulator such as the ZOC Terminal Emulator, it is possible to perform text-based communication with the BYOC CPU. See Appendix G for ZOC terminal setup. The Cyclone V GX Starter Kit User Manual provides configuration information including pin numbers for all components and devices. For example, the right-most red LED's pin number is PIN_F7. Using the Quartus Pin Planner, AReg[0] is assigned to PIN_F7 as shown below. The remaining AReg bits are assigned to other red LEDs.

Node Name	Direction	Location	I/O Bank	VREF Group	Fitter Location	I/O Stand
AReg[5]	Output	PIN_J7	8A	B8A_N0	PIN_J7	2.5 V
AReg[4]	Output	PIN_J8	8A	B8A_N0	PIN_J8	2.5 V
AReg[3]	Output	PIN_G7	8A	B8A_N0	PIN_G7	2.5 V
AReg[2]	Output	PIN_G6	8A	B8A_N0	PIN_G6	2.5 V
AReg[1]	Output	PIN_F6	8A	B8A_N0	PIN_F6	2.5 V
AReg[0]	Output	PIN_F7	8A	B8A_N0	PIN_F7	2.5 V
out _	Output				PIN T1 1	2 5 V (d-f

In the next chapter, I test the Cyclone V FPGA and put it through its paces.

Chapter 11 – Testing the FPGA BYOC CPU

Because of the increased complexity of FPGAs, functional simulation is first used to test the design. This involves simulating inputs including the system clock and then checking that the resulting outputs are as expected. Most of the Excel Assembler "Basic Test" folder programs can serve as tests for this purpose. Once completed, actual hardware tests using the same programs can be done.

Functional Testing

Functional testing is done using the "University Program" simulation tool available in Quartus. There are dozens of videos describing how to use the tool. The one by Professor Kleitz is accessed here[7].

To illustrate its use, consider the Test Code 1 program listed below.

---

[7] https://www.youtube.com/watch?v=a8JAkKhxlQl

```
;
;Test Code 1
;
; Basic Counting 1
; d=1;a=5 4 3 2 1 0 5...
;
start:                  mvi        a,1
                        mov        d,a
                        mvi        a,5
loop:                   sub        a,d
                        bnz        loop
                        jmp        start
```

After assembling the program, the BYOC-PROM.MIF file is updated with the resulting object code. See Appendix A for more information. The system clock pre-counter (component C0) is not needed for the simulation. Rather than removing it, the SysClk input to the Clock Unit is changed temporarily to "sysclk". These are the steps for functional simulation.

Step 1. Compile the project.

Step 2. From the Quartus main menu, select File—New—Verification/Debugging Files—University Program VWF.

Step 3. From the Simulation Waveform Editor, select File—Open.

Step 4. Navigate to the Waveform.vwf file in the project folder and open it. The test waveform will appear.

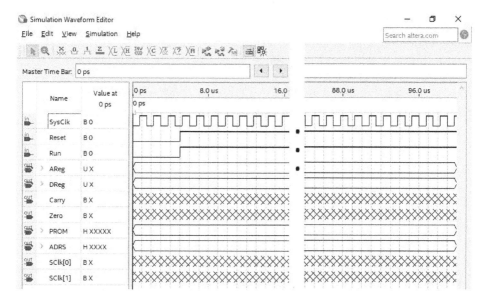

The horizontal scale is time 0 to 100 microseconds. Along the left side are BYOC inputs and outputs. Input SysClk is configured as a 1 microsecond period square wave (50% duty cycle). Inputs Reset (low active) and Run are "0" until 5 microseconds then they become "1" beginning execution. The displayed radix for each output is selectable. "B" is binary; "U" is unsigned decimal; and "H" is hexadecimal.

To run the simulation, select Simulation—Run Functional Simulation. The waveform below is the result.

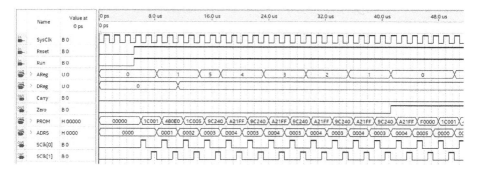

As addresses (ADRS) and program instructions (PROM) change, the values in registers A and D change as they should. If this were not the case, inspecting the other outputs could help with troubleshooting.

Not all outputs are simulated in the test waveform above. Three additional ones (OP0, OP1, and ALUR) would be very helpful in troubleshooting because their values are well defined for nearly all instructions. Follow these steps, to include other outputs.

Step 1. From the Simulation Waveform Editor select Edit—Insert—Insert Node or Bus. This window will appear.

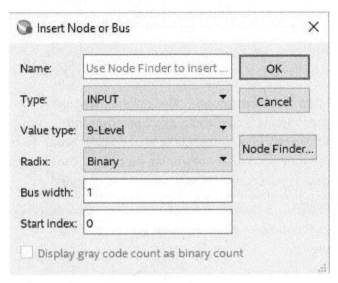

Step 2. Click Node Finder to see this.

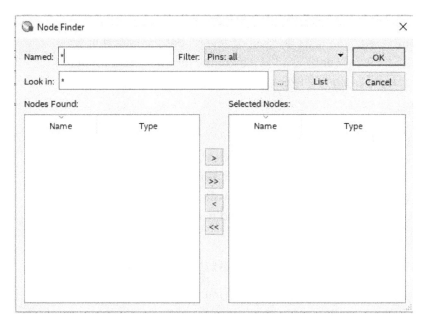

Step 3. Click List and move output groups ALUR, OP0, and OP1 to the Selected Nodes window. Click OK twice.

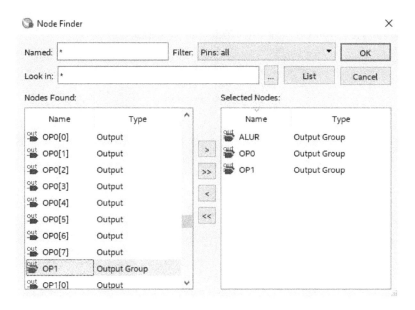

157

Eventually all the test programs in the Excel Basic Tests folder were functionally simulated. The tests uncovered several design flaws that were corrected. With the confidence level at a high, the hardware test using the GX Starter Board and Cyclone V FPGA was next.

Hardware Testing

As already noted, pin assignments include both the A register (red LEDs) and the D resister (green LEDs). Most of the Basic Test programs produce results with these two registers and therefore are satisfactory for preliminary hardware tests. The steps below program and test the Cyclone Y FPGA with the Test Code 1.

Step 1. Assemble the test program then update the BYOC-PROM.MIF file.

Step 2. Change the SysClk input to the Clock Unit to q[20] to slow the CPU sufficiently so that the register value changes in the LEDs are slow enough to be seen.

Step 3. Compile the project.

Step 4. Click Tools-Programmer to see the Programmer window.

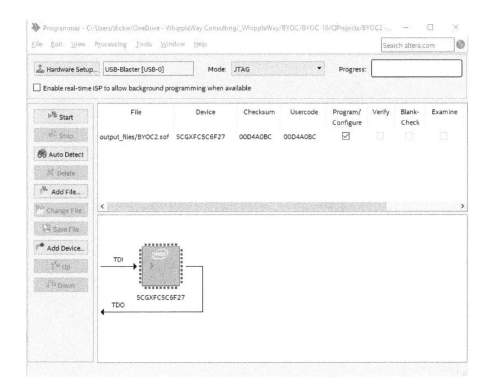

If the Start button is greyed out, click Hardware Setup…

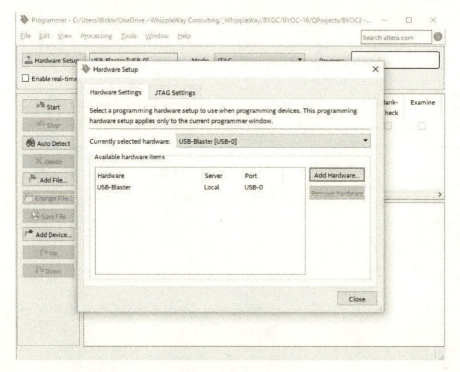

If USB-Blaster[USB-0] does not show in the "Currently selected hardware" box, click the box and select it.

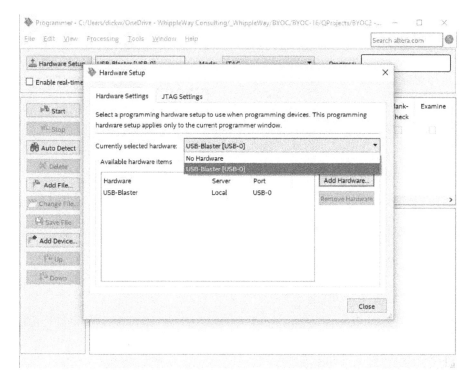

Step 5. Click Close and OK. Then Click Start. When the Progress indicator reaches 100%, the program has downloaded.

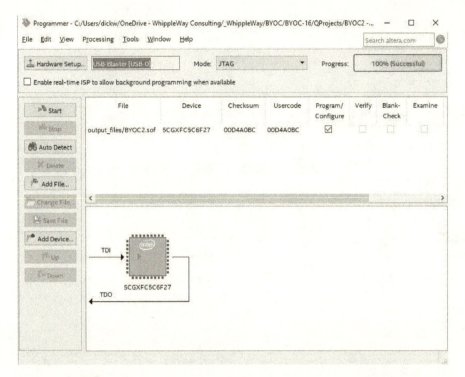

Step 6. Press the Reset button (KEY3) and raise the Run switch to the up position. The green LEDs will show a binary 1 and the red LEDs will count in binary from 5 to 0 and repeat. The two left-most red LEDs indicate subclocks T0 and T1.

The remaining tests follow a similar procedure. To change programs, it is not necessary to re-compile the project. Instead, follow these steps.

Step 1. From the Quartus main screen, select "Processing—Update Memory Initialization File".

Step 2. When finished, select "Processing—Start—Start Assembler"

The FPGA is ready to program with the new program. The "Hello World" program displays its message on the ZOC terminal. The "Hello World" text is stored in the Data ROM (DROM). After updating the program in BYOC-PROM.MIF, copy and paste the assembler's Data Rom object code into BYOC-

DROM.MIF. Use the steps above to update memory. After programming the FPGA, unplug the Blaster USB and plug in the Serial USB. Use ZOC "File-Quick Start" to initialize the terminal. Reset the CPU and switch to RUN. The display should display, "Hello World". Both the Number Guess and Life programs work best with the SysClk input on the Clock Unit set to q[8]. In fact, the Life program running at top speed produces generations too fast for the ZOC terminal emulation. Recall that Logisim took 3 minutes to compute one Life generation. Tests of the Life program with q[0] produced 68 generations per second! The Cyclone V was executing an amazing 12.5 million instructions per second. The figure below shows the first four Life generations.

```
     *
    ***
    * *
    ***
     *
```

```
   ***
   * *
  *     *
   * *
   ***
```

Gen 1

Gen 2

```
    *
   * *
  ** **
  ** **
  ** **
   * *
    *
```

```
     *
  **   **

  *       *

  **   **
     *
```

Gen 3

Gen 4

In the last chapter, I consider what has been accomplished and perhaps what is next.

Chapter 12 – What's Next

From the basic theory of AND, OR, and NOT logic, a working computer was first simulated then implemented in hardware. Interestingly, the hardware version of the BYOC CPU used less than 2% of the available Cyclone V's ALMs (Adaptive Logic Modules), the basic building blocks of the FPGA. Building a working computer with so few of its resources suggests what a powerful tool the FPGA is for creative logic design.

As to the question of "What's next?", one answer could be to design an even more powerful processor. With all the commercially available processors, this would seem unnecessary. But what if the FPGA design were to target a specific application to take advantage of speed and programming simplicity. That might be a worthwhile pursuit. In which case, the BYOC CPU could be a starting point for such a project.

In the final analysis, the goal of the BYOC project was to gain a better understanding of how computers work. That I hope the reader can say has been a result. Additional Information including software downloads is available at the author's website http://www.whippleway.com.

Appendix A – Excel Assembler

Assembler Basics

Writing machine code by hand is tedious and time consuming. Programmers use a software application called an *assembler* to translate assembly instructions into machine code. Assembly instructions take the form of human readable text referred to as *source code*. The machine or *object code*, on the other hand, takes a variety of different forms ranging from binary to hex formatted text. Both Logisim and Quartus provide an option to use hex formatted text and that is the one used with the BYOC project.

Assemblers are usually written in languages like Java or C++. For expediency and ease of development, the choice for the BYOC project was Microsoft Excel. The source code is entered as a column of text and then Visual BASIC for Applications that is embedded in Excel does the translation to object code.

Reviewing the example assembly program below and the comments that follow will help explain how to use the Excel assembler.

Program Source/Object Code

The figure below shows the program section of the worksheet including the source and assembled object code. Explanation of the various components continue below the figure.

166

Label	Operation	Operand	Comment	Label	Instruction	Address	Logisim Object Code	Quartus MIF Code		
;				START:	CALL CLR_SCR	00	D000A	0 : D000A;		Assemble
; Program Begin					MVI D,HI(MSG0)	01	08000	1 : 08000;		
;					MVI E,LO(MSG0)	02	0C000	2 : 0C000;		
start:	call	clr_scr	;Clear display		CALL MOUT	03	D000E	3 : D000E;		
	mvi	d,hi(msg0)	;Display message		CALL NEW_LINE	04	D000C	4 : D000C;		
	mvi	e,lo(msg0)			MVI D,HI(MSG1)	05	08000	5 : 08000;		
	call	mout			MVI E,LO(MSG1)	06	0C00C	6 : 0C00C;		
	call	new_line	;New line		CALL MOUT	07	D000E	7 : D000E;		
	mvi	d,hi(msg1)	;Display message		CALL NEW_LINE	08	D000C	8 : D000C;		
	mvi	e,lo(msg1)		SELF:	JMP SELF	09	F0009	9 : F0009;		
	call	mout		CLR_SCR:	MVI B,CNTR_L	0A	0000C	10 : 0000C;		
	call	new_line	;New line		JMP BOUT	0B	F0016	11 : F0016;		
self:	jmp	self	;Done	NEW_LINE:	MVI B,EOL	0C	0000A	12 : 0000A;		
;					JMP BOUT	0D	F0016	13 : F0016;		
; Clear Screen Routine				MOUT:	LROM B	0E	60000	14 : 60000;		
;					OR B,B	0F	81900	15 : 81900;		
clr_scr:	mvi	b,cntr_l	;Display clear screen character		BZ MOUT_DONE	10	A0005	16 : A0005;		
	jmp	bout			CALL BOUT	11	D0016	17 : D0016;		

1. Row 1 contains the column headers. Program source code is entered in columns A to D. E to G is the assembly listing. H is the Logisim object code and I is the Quartus object code. Click the "Assemble" button to assemble the source code.

2. Start the source code in cell A2 as shown.

3. A semicolon leftmost in Column A indicates a comment line that is ignored by the assembler. Column D is also reserved for comments. A semicolon here is not needed but is advised for future compatibility with another assembler.

4. Columns A to D reserved for the assembly source code. Column A is for an optional label always followed by a colon; B for the operation; C for operands; and D for optional comments. Source code may be entered in lower or upper case and will be translated to upper case in the assembled listing.

5. Column E is the label for the assembled listing. F is the assembled operation with its operands. G is the assembled address in hex. Comments are ignored in the assembled listing.

6. Column H is the 20-bit hex listing of the assembled PROM code that can be copied and pasted into the Logisim PROM editor.

7. Column I is the decimal address and 20-bit hex listing of the assembled PROM code that can be copied and pasted into a Quartus MIF file.

Note: Program ROM storage begins at address 0x0000 and increments for each instruction.

Data Source Code

The figure below shows the data section of the worksheet that follows the program section. Its components are explained below the figure.

● ● ●

	A	B	C	D	E	F
46		ret		;Return to calling program		
47	;					
48	; End Program - Begin Data Section					
49	;					
50	data					
51	;					
52	; Variable Equates					
53	;					
54	rsze	equ	256		;	
55	cr	equ	13		Label/Variable	Value
56	lf	equ	10		START	0
57	eol	equ	10		SELF	9
58	cntr_l	equ	12		CLR_SCR	10
59	bs	equ	8		NEW_LINE	12
60	buf_start	equ	0		MOUT	14
61	cntr_port	equ	4		MOUT_DONE	21
62	data_port	equ	5		BOUT	22
63	;				BOUT_0	23
64	; Messages in Data ROM (DROM)				RSZE	256
65	;				CR	13
66	msg0:	Hello World			LF	10
67	msg1:	db	72,101,108,108,111,32,87,111,114,108,100,0		EOL	10
68	;				CNTR_L	12
69	; Address space in Data RAM (DRAM)				BS	8
70	;				BUF_START	0
71	rstrt	equ	0		CNTR_PORT	4
72	rend	equ	rstrt+rsze		DATA_PORT	5
73	;				MSG0	0
74	; End Data Section				MSG1	12
75	;				RSTRT	0
76	end				REND	256

8. Beginning after the end of the program section is the data section. A "data" statement in column A (row 50 in the example) marks the beginning of the data section. The data section consists of three data types:

   a. Variable Equates – Variables are useful for storing values that may change in differing situations. They also help in self-documenting the code. Refer to rows 54 to 62. Column A contains the variable name that must begin with a letter.

168

Remaining characters can be letters, numerals 0 to 9, hyphens, and underscores. There is no length restriction. Column B is the "equ" operator. Column C is the value to be assigned to the variable. It can be an algebraic expression involving numeric constants and previously defined labels and variables.

b. Text Strings – Text strings to be stored in the Data ROM must begin with an identifying label in column A. The text string is in column B. Use an underscore character to continue text to the next row. A zero byte is automatically added to denote the end of the string. See row 66 for example.

c. Data Bytes – Numeric data can be stored in the Data ROM using the "db" operator. A label in column A indicates the address of the first byte. The "db" operator is in column B. Data bytes are in column C with their values in a list separated by commas. Values can be in decimal, binary, or hex format. See row 67 for example.

Note: Data ROM storage begins at 0x0000 with the first text character or data byte defined and increments continuously with each added text character or data byte.

9. The last line of the source code must have an "end" statement in column A (row 76 in the example).
10. In columns E and F is a list of label/variable names and their assembled values. These can be useful when troubleshooting a program.

Data (DROM) Object Code

As shown in the figure below, data object code generated from the data section is listed just past the end of the program object code (row 31 in the example). Column H is formatted for Logisim while column I for Quartus.

	A	B	C	D	E	F	G	H	I
29		or	b,b	;End of message?		POP A	18	9F800	27 : 9F800;
30		bz	mout_done	;If so, done		RET	1C	C0000	28 : C0000;
31		call	bout	;Otherwise, output B	MSG0:		0	48	0 : 48;
32		inr	e	;Next byte			1	65	1 : 65;
33		inz	d				2	6C	2 : 6C;
34		jmp	mout	;Do again			3	6C	3 : 6C;
35	;						4	6F	4 : 6F;
36	mout_done:	ret		;Return to calling program			5	20	5 : 20;
37	;						6	57	6 : 57;
38	; Output Single Character in B						7	6F	7 : 6F;
39	;						8	72	8 : 72;
40	bout:	push	a	;Save A			9	6C	9 : 6C;
41	bout_0:	inp	a,cntr_port	;Get control byte			10	64	10 : 64;
42		ani	a,128	;Display busy?			11	00	11 : 00;
43		bnz	bout_0	;If so, wait	MSG1:		12	48	12 : 48;
44		out	data_port,b	;Otherwise Output B			13	65	13 : 65;
45		pop	a	;Restore A			14	6C	14 : 6C;
46		ret		;Return to calling program			15	6C	15 : 6C;
47	;						16	6F	16 : 6F;
48	; End Program - Begin Data Section						17	20	17 : 20;
49	;						18	57	18 : 57;
50	data						19	6F	19 : 6F;
51	;						20	72	20 : 72;
52	; Variable Equates						21	6C	21 : 6C;
53	;						22	64	22 : 64;
54	rsze	equ	256		;				

The VBA assembler targets the active worksheet. To create a new program worksheet, copy an existing program worksheet and modify as needed. To do this, hover over the existing program worksheet's tab and right click. Choose "Move or Copy" than check the "Create a copy" box and click "OK".

Logisim Programming

The following steps load program and data object code into the Logisim BYOC:

1. Assemble the program.

2. Select and copy the program object code in the Logisim column H.

E	F	G	H
Label	Instruction	Address	Logisim Object Code
START:	MVI D,HI(MSG0)	00	08000
	MVI E,LO(MSG0)	01	0C000
LOOP:	LROM B	02	60000
	OR B,B	03	81900
DONE:	BZ DONE	04	A0000
	CALL BOUT	05	D0009
	INR E	06	8D000
	INZ D	07	89200
	JMP LOOP	08	F0002
BOUT:	PUSH A	09	9F000
BOUT_0:	INP A,CNTR_PORT	0A	9F904
	ANI A,128	0B	3D880
	BNZ BOUT_0	0C	A21FE
	OUT DATA_PORT,B	0D	83105
	POP A	0E	9F800
	RET	0F	C0000
MSG0:		0	48

3. In the Logisim Hex Editor for the Program ROM, select the first byte and paste the program code.

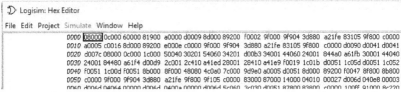

4. Back to the assembled code, select and copy the data object code following the program object code.

	OUT DATA_PORT,B	0D	83105
	POP A	0E	9F800
	RET	0F	C0000
MSG0:		0	48
		1	65
		2	6C
		3	6C
		4	6F
		5	20
		6	57
		7	6F
		8	72
		9	6C
		10	64
		11	00

5. In the Logisim Hex Editor for the Data ROM, select the first byte and paste the data object code.

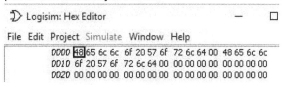

6. The program is ready to run.

Quartus Programming

The following steps load program and data object code into the Quartus BYOC:

1. Assemble the program.
2. Select and copy the program object code in the Logisim column I.

E	F	G	H	I
Label	Instruction	Address	Logisim Object Code	Quartus MIF Code
START:	MVI D,HI(MSG0)	00	08000	0 : 08000;
	MVI E,LO(MSG0)	01	0C000	1 : 0C000;
LOOP:	LROM B	02	60000	2 : 60000;
	OR B,B	03	81900	3 : 81900;
DONE:	BZ DONE	04	A0000	4 : A0000;
	CALL BOUT	05	D0009	5 : D0009;
	INR E	06	8D000	6 : 8D000;
	INZ D	07	89200	7 : 89200;
	JMP LOOP	08	F0002	8 : F0002;
BOUT:	PUSH A	09	9F000	9 : 9F000;
BOUT_0:	INP A,CNTR_PORT	0A	9F904	10 : 9F904;
	ANI A,128	0B	3D880	11 : 3D880;
	BNZ BOUT_0	0C	A21FE	12 : A21FE;
	OUT DATA_PORT,B	0D	83105	13 : 83105;
	POP A	0E	9F800	14 : 9F800;
	RET	0F	C0000	15 : C0000;
MSG0:		0	48	0 : 48;

3. Using a text editor, open the project file BYOC-PROM.MIF. Paste the program object code into the area between the "CONTENT BEGIN" line and the "[xx..4095] : 0" line. Change the "xx" to the number of the last byte of the program plus one (16 in this case). Save the

file.

```
BYOC-DROM.mif    BYOC-PROM.mif

 1   -- Copyright (C) 2017  Intel Corporation. All rights reserved.
 2   -- Your use of Intel Corporation's design tools, logic functions
 3   -- and other software and tools, and its AMPP partner logic
 4   -- functions, and any output files from any of the foregoing
 5   -- (including device programming or simulation files), and any
 6   -- associated documentation or information are expressly subject
 7   -- to the terms and conditions of the Intel Program License
 8   -- Subscription Agreement, the Intel Quartus Prime License Agreement,
 9   -- the Intel FPGA IP License Agreement, or other applicable license
10   -- agreement, including, without limitation, that your use is for
11   -- the sole purpose of programming logic devices manufactured by
12   -- Intel and sold by Intel or its authorized distributors.  Please
13   -- refer to the applicable agreement for further details.
14
15   -- Quartus Prime generated Memory Initialization File (.mif)
16
17   WIDTH=20;
18   DEPTH=4096;
19
20   ADDRESS_RADIX=UNS;
21   DATA_RADIX=HEX;
22
23   CONTENT BEGIN
24   |
25        0    :    08000;
26        1    :    0C000;
27        2    :    60000;
28        3    :    81900;
29        4    :    A0000;
30        5    :    D0009;
31        6    :    8D000;
32        7    :    89200;
33        8    :    F0002;
34        9    :    9F000;
35       10    :    9F904;
36       11    :    3D880;
37       12    :    A21FE;
38       13    :    83105;
39       14    :    9F800;
40       15    :    C0000;
41
42      [16..4095]  :    00;
```

4. Back to the assembled code, select and copy the data object code following the program object code.

	OUT DATA_PORT,B	0D	83105		13 :	83105;
	POP A	0E	9F800		14 :	9F800;
	RET	0F	C0000		15 :	C0000;
MSG0:		0	48		0 :	48;
		1	65		1 :	65;
		2	6C		2 :	6C;
		3	6C		3 :	6C;
		4	6F		4 :	6F;
		5	20		5 :	20;
		6	57		6 :	57;
		7	6F		7 :	6F;
		8	72		8 :	72;
		9	6C		9 :	6C;
		10	64		10 :	64;
		11	00		11 :	00;

173

5. Using a text editor, open the project file BYOC-DROM.MIF. Paste the data object code into the area between the "CONTENT BEGIN" line and the "[xx..1023] : 0" line. Change the "xx" to the number of the last byte of the program plus one (12 in this case). Save the file.

```
BYOC-DROM.mif    BYOC-PROM.mif
  1   -- Copyright (C) 2017  Intel Corporation. All rights reserved.
  2   -- Your use of Intel Corporation's design tools, logic functions
  3   -- and other software and tools, and its AMPP partner logic
  4   -- functions, and any output files from any of the foregoing
  5   -- (including device programming or simulation files), and any
  6   -- associated documentation or information are expressly subject
  7   -- to the terms and conditions of the Intel Program License
  8   -- Subscription Agreement, the Intel Quartus Prime License Agreement,
  9   -- the Intel FPGA IP License Agreement, or other applicable license
 10   -- agreement, including, without limitation, that your use is for
 11   -- the sole purpose of programming logic devices manufactured by
 12   -- Intel and sold by Intel or its authorized distributors.  Please
 13   -- refer to the applicable agreement for further details.
 14
 15   -- Quartus Prime generated Memory Initialization File (.mif)
 16
 17   WIDTH=8;
 18   DEPTH=1024;
 19
 20   ADDRESS_RADIX=UNS;
 21   DATA_RADIX=HEX;
 22
 23   CONTENT BEGIN
 24
 25            0    :    48;
 26            1    :    65;
 27            2    :    6C;
 28            3    :    6C;
 29            4    :    6F;
 30            5    :    20;
 31            6    :    57;
 32            7    :    6F;
 33            8    :    72;
 34            9    :    6C;
 35           10    :    64;
 36           11    :    00;
 37
 38         [12..1023]  :   00;
 39   END;
```

6. The program is ready to download and run.

Appendix B - Quartus Symbol Tool

The Symbol Tool is found on the Quartus Block Edit bar. Clicking it brings up the Symbol catalog. In it are two libraries. The first is the Project library containing any symbols created from the IP Catalog for the current project. The second is an Intel library containing a large and varied selection of useful devices. After selecting a device from either library and clicking "OK", the symbol for the device can be dragged and dropped into a circuit.

The Intel library contains a "primitives" folder with the basic gates like AND, OR, XOR, and NOT. Also, in the library is a "Megafunctions" folder containing a wide range of more complex devices. For instance, there is a multiplexer LPM_MUX essentially the same as the IP Catalog device described in Appendix C. It is not necessary to create the device from scratch as with the IP Catalog. Once selected, a basically configured device can be dragged and dropped into a circuit. To change the configuration, right click the device and select "Parameters". This form appears.

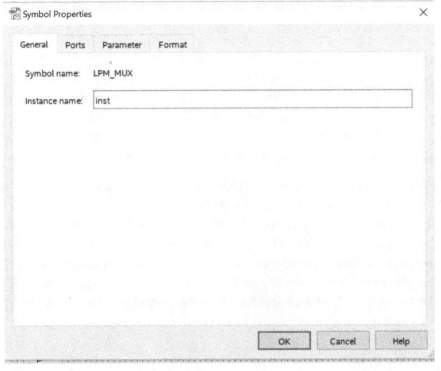

Enter the instance name then click on the "Ports" tab to see this form.

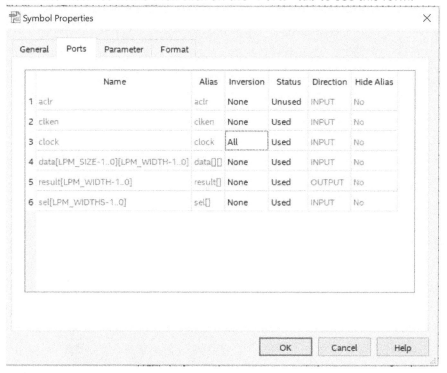

To invert an Input or Output, double click the "Inversion" column and select "Invert" to invert all bits of the port. For the Status column, double click an Input or Output and choose the "Unused" option to disable it. In the example above, the "aclr" input is disabled and the "clock" input is inverted.

Next, click the "Parameter" tab.

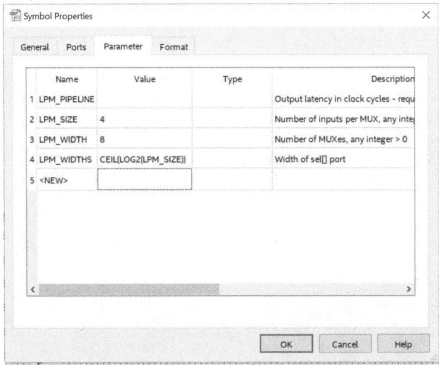

The non-grayed out items can be changed. For the multiplexer, double click the "LPM_SIZE" and "LPM_WIDTH" Values to configure the multiplexer to desired size and width (4 and 8 respectively in this instance). The resulting multiplexer functions now are the same as the IP Catalog device in Appendix C. For additional information see the Intel LPM Reference Guide is available here[8].

---

[8]
https://www.intel.com/content/dam/www/programmable/us/en/pdfs/literature/catalogs/lpm.pdf

Appendix C – Quartus IP Catalog

The IP (Intellectual Property) Catalog contains many useful devices but they must be created and configured. As an example, follow these steps to create a four input by 8-bit wide multiplexer:

1. From the Quartus main screen, select Tools—IP Catalog.
2. In the IP Catalog search window, type "mux".

3. Double click "LPM_MUX".
4. Complete the pop-up form by (a) entering the name of the new device – "mux4x8" and (b) checking the VHDL box. Click OK. This is my naming convention read "mux 4 inputs by 8 wide".

5. A series of forms appears. From the first, enter the number of inputs "4" and the width as "8". Click "Next".

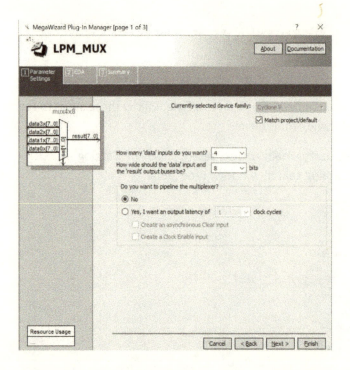

6. Click "Next" again to skip the Simulation Libraries form.
7. On the Files form, check the "bsf" file type. The "cmp" file type should already be checked.

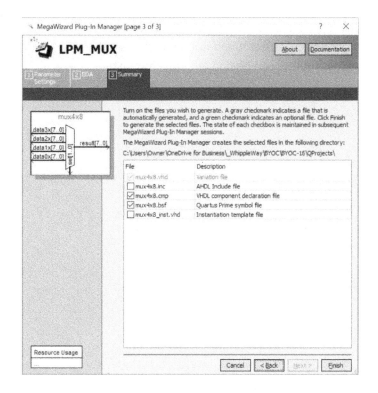

8. Click "Finish".

Double click in any blank circuit area and the Symbol form will appear. The new multiplexer will appear in the project library ready for use.

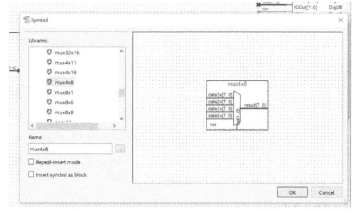

To edit an existing IP device, select it and double click. The same series of forms appear and parameters can be changed for that instance only.

Appendix D – Sieve of Eratosthenes[9]

The following is listing of the Sieve of Eratosthenes written for the Logisim BYOC CPM:

Label	Operation	Operand	Comment
;			
; Sieve of Eratosthenes			
;			
; Generate Primes on range 1 to 100			
;			
; Fill the first 100 locations of RAM with values 1 to 100.			
;			
start:	call	clr_scr	;Clear screen
	mvi	d,hi(msg0)	;Display title
	mvi	e,lo(msg0)	
	call	mout	
	call	new_line	;Skip a line
	call	new_line	
	mvi	l,100	;HL is the pointer to DRAM
	mvi	h,0	
	mvi	e,100	;E is max value
loop0:	mov	m,e	;Store value
	dcr	l	;Decrement address
	dcr	e	;Decrement value
	bnz	loop0	;If value not zero, do again
;			

---

[9] Electronic copies of all programs are available via my website www.whippleway.com.

183

```
;   Zero all multiple locations up to Square Root(100) = 10
;
              mvi      c,2          ;Start with 2 as base value
                                    ;Set DRAM pointer to address
loop1:        mov      l,c          of base value
                                    ;Has the base value been
              or       m,m          stricken?
                                    ;If so, move on to next value to
              bz       next_n       strike
                                    ;Otherwise, compute address of
loop2:        add      l,c          multiple
              mvi      m,0          ;Zero location to strike
                                    ;Have multiples 100 or less
              cpi      l,101        been  stricken?
              bc       loop2        ;If not, strike another
next_n:       inr      c            ;Otherwise, next base value
              cpi      c,10         ;Reached 10?
                                    ;If not, do multiple zeroing
              bnz      loop1        again
;
;   Display Primes in First 100 bytes of MRAM
;
              mvi      l,2          ;Start at location 2
              mvi      h,0
loop3:        or       m,m          ;Is value zero?
              bz       dspl_next    ;If so, display next value
              mov      e,m          ;Move prime to DE
              mvi      d,0
cont2:        call     dout         ;Display DE
              mvi      b,space
              call     bout
dspl_next
:             inr      l            ;Pointer to next n
```

184

```
            cpi     l,100           ;Past last prime?
            bc      loop3           ;If not, do again
self:       jmp     self            ;Done
;
; Covert Number in DE to ASCII and Display It
;
;   L is used as flag to suppress output of leading zeros except when
D is zero.
;
dout:       push    l               ;Save HL
            push    h
            mvi     l,0             ;Zero suppression flag
            mvi     b,0             ;Zero hundreds counter
                                    ;Pass position bias (100) to
            mvi     c,100           convert subroutine
            call    cnvrt           ;Display hundreds digit
            mvi     b,0             ;Zero tens counter
                                    ;Pass position bias (10) to
            mvi     c,10            convert subroutine
            call    cnvrt           ;Display tens digit
            mov     b,e             ;Display remainder as ones digit
            adi     b,48            ;Add ASCII bias
            call    bout            ;Display ones digit on TTY
            pop     h               ;Restore HL
            pop     l
            ret                     ;Done-return to calling routine
;
; Display Positional Digit in DE
;
                                    ;Set zero suppress auxilliary flag
cnvrt:      mvi     h,255           to -1
cnvrt_0:    inr     h               ;Increment it
            sub     e,c             ;Subtract position bias from DE
```

185

```
                sbb         d,b
                                        ;If result positive, subtract bias
                bnc         cnvrt_0     again
                add         e,c         ;Otherwise, add bias back to DE
                adc         d,b
                cmp         h,l         ;Is result zero?
                bnz         cnvrt_1     ;If not, display it
                                        ;Otherwise, just return
                ret                     displaying
cnvrt_1:        dcr         l           ;Turn off zero suppression
                mov         b,h         ;Add ASCII bias then display it
                adi         b,48
                jmp         bout
;
;  Output Single Character in B
;
bout:           push        a           ;Save A
bout_0:         inp         a,cntr_port ;Is TTY busy
                ani         a,128
                bnz         bout_0      ;If so, wait
                            data_port,
                out         b           ;Otherwise, display character
                pop         a           ;Restore A
                ret                     ;Return to calling routine
;
;  Output New Line Routine
;
new_line:       mvi         b,eol       ;Display new line character
                jmp         bout
;
;  Clear Screen
Routine
;
```

```
clr_scr:    mvi     b,cntr_l        ;Display clear screen character
            jmp     bout
;
;  Output Message at DE IN DROM
Routine
;
;  Message terminates with 0x00
byte
;
                                    ;Get first message byte from
mout:       lrom    b               DROM
            or      b,b             ;Is it zero?
                    mout_don
            bz      e               ;If so, done
            call    bout            ;Otherwise, display it
            inr     e               ;Increment DE
            inz     d
            jmp     mout            ;Do again
mout_do
ne:         ret
;
;  End of Program and beginning of
data
;
data
;
eol         equ             13  ;End-of-line character
cntr_l      equ             12  ;Control L - clear screen
space       equ             32  ;Space character
cntr_port   equ              4  ;Terminal Unit control port
data_port   equ              5  ;Terminal Unit data port
;
```

```
                Sieve of Eratosthenes
msg0:       - 100                          ;Title message
;
;  End of
data
;
end
```

Appendix E – High/Low Number Guess

The following is listing of the Number Guess written for the Logisim BYOC CPM:

```
;

;  Set-Up Code
;
setup:          call    clr_scr         ;Clear screen
                mvi     h,hi(msg0)      ;Display title
                mvi     l,lo(msg0)
                call    mout

;
;  Main Code
;
main:           call    new_line        ;Skip line
                call    new_line
                mvi     h,hi(msg1)      ;Display instructions
                mvi     l,lo(msg1)
                call    mout
                call    new_line        ;Next line
                mvi     h,hi(msg2)      ;Continue display instructions
                mvi     l,lo(msg2)
                call    mout
;               mvi     e,50
                call    get_rnd_num     ;Get random value 1 to 100 in E
                mvi     d,0             ;Zero try counter D
get_guess:      call    new_line        ;Next line
                mvi     h,hi(msg3)      ;Display guess request
                mvi     l,lo(msg3)
                call    mout
```

```
              call    buf_in          ;Get guess into buffer
              inr     d               ;Increment D, try counter
              call    cinp            ;Get guess into C from buffer
              cmp     c,e             ;Compare guess C to value in E?
              bz      got_it          ;If equal, branch to Got It
                                      ;If guess C greater than E,
              bnc     high            branch to high
                                      ;Otherwise, display low
low:          mvi     h,hi(msg7)      message
              mvi     l,lo(msg7)
finish:       call    mout
              jmp     get_guess       ;Do again
                                      Display high message and do
high:         mvi     h,hi(msg6)      again
              mvi     l,lo(msg6)
              jmp     finish
                                      ;Display Got It message and
got_it:       mvi     h,hi(msg4)      number tries
              mvi     l,lo(msg4)
              call    mout
              call    dout            ;Display number of tries in D
              mvi     h,hi(msg5)
              mvi     l,lo(msg5)
              call    mout
              jmp     main            ;Do over from main entry point
;
;  Buffer Input Routine
;
buf_in:       mvi     h,hi(buf_start) ;Point HL to start of buffer
              mvi     l,lo(buf_start)
              mvi     c,0             ;Buffered characters count
                                      ;Get a charater in B and display
buf_in_0:     call    bin             it
              cpi     b,bs
```

```
                    bnz     buf_in_2          ;If not, continue...
                    or      c,c               ;At buffer start?
                                              ;If so, do nothing and get next
                    bz      buf_in_0          character
                                              ;Otherwise, position back one
                    dcr     c                 character
                    or      l,l               ;Is L zero?
                    bnz     buf_in_1          ;If so, H must be decremented
                    dcr     h                 ;Along with L
buf_in_1:           dcr     l                 ;Point back one character
                    jmp     buf_in_0          ;Get next character
buf_in_2:           mov     m,b               ;Save at HL
                    inr     c                 ;Position next character
                    inr     l                 ;Increment HL
                    bnz     buf_in_3
                    inr     h
buf_in_3:           cpi     b,eol             ;Check for end ofline character
                    bnz     buf_in_0          ;If not, do again
                    ret                       ;Otherwise, done and return
;
;  Clear Screen Routine
;
                                              ;Display Control-L, clear screen
clr_scr:            mvi     b,cntr_l          character
                    jmp     bout
;
;  Display New Line
Routine
;
new_line:           mvi     b,eol             ;Display new line character
                    jmp     bout
;
;  Display Message at HL Routine (terminates with 0x00)
```

```
;
mout:          push   d              Save D
               push   e              Save E
               mov    d,h            ;Move HL to DE
               mov    e,l
mout0:         lrom   b              ;Get character at DE into B
               or     b,b            ;Is it zero?
               bz     mout_done      ;If so, done and exit
               call   bout           ;Otherwise, display it
               inr    e              ;Point next DE
               inz    d
               jmp    mout0          ;Do again
mout_done:     pop    e              ;Restore E
               pop    d              ;Restore D
               ret                   ;Return
;
;  Input Single Character to B from
Keyboard
;
bin:           push   a              ;Save A
bin_0:         inp    a,cntr_port    ;Get control status into A
               ani    a,0b01000000   ;Is a character available?
               bz     bin_0          ;If not, wait
                                     ;Otherwise, get the character
               inp    b,data_port    into B
               pop    a              ;Restore A
;
;  Output Single
Character in B
;
bout:          push   a              ;Save A
bout_0:        inp    a,cntr_port    ;Get control status into A
               ani    a,0b10000000   ;Is display busy?
```

```
                bnz     bout_0              ;If so, wait
                out     data_port,b         Otherwise, output it
                pop     a                   ;Restore A
                ret                         ;Return
;
; Get Random Number 0 to 100 in E
;
get_rnd_num:    call    new_line            ;New line
                                            ;Point HL to 'Press any key..."
                mvi     h,0                 message
                mvi     l,msg8
                call    mout                ;Display message
get_rnd_num_
0:              inp     a,cntr_port         ;Get keyboard control byte
                ani     a,64                ;Is character available?
                        get_rnd_num_
                bz      0                   ;If not, keep checking
                                            ;Otherwise, clear keyboard data
                inp     a,data_port         port
                inp     e,rnd_port          ;Get random value into E
get_rnd_num_
1:              sui     e,101               ;Compute modulo 100
                        get_rnd_num_
                bnc     1
                adi     e,101
                ret                         ;Return to calling routine
;
;  Convert Number in D to ASCII and
display
;
;    L is used as flag to suppress display of leading zeros except when D is
zero.
;
dout:           mvi     l,0                 ;Zero suppression flag
```

193

```
                                    ;Pass digit value (100) to
            mvi     e,100           convert routine
            call    cnvrt           ;Display 100s digit
                                    ;Pass digit value (10) to convert
            mvi     e,10            routine
            call    cnvrt           ;Display 10s digit
            mov     b,d             ;Display 1s digit
            adi     b,48            ;Add ASCII bias
            jmp     bout            ;Output it
;
cnvrt:      mvi     h,255           ;Preset H as zero surpress flag
cnvrt_0:    inr     h               ;Increment it
            sub     d,e             ;Subtract digit value
            bnc     cnvrt_0         ;If no borow do, do again
            add     d,e             ;Otherwise, add digit value back
                                    ;Is digit to be displayed equal to
            cmp     h,l             suppress flag?
            bnz     cnvrt_1         ;If not, display it
                                    ;Otherwise, return without
            ret                     display
cnvrt_1:    dcr     l               ;Turn off zero surpress flag
            mov     b,h             ;Get character to display into B
            adi     b,48            ;Add ASCII bias
            jmp     bout            ;Output it
;
;   Convert ASCII number at BUF_START to binary in C
;
cinp:       mvi     c,0             ;Preset C for single digit result
            mvi     h,hi(buf_start) ;Point HL to start of buffer
            mvi     l,lo(buf_start)
            mov     b,m             ;Get ASCII character
            cpi     a,eol           ;Is it the end-of-line?
            bz      cinp_2          If so, done and exit.
```

194

```
cinp_0:          sui    b,48         ;Otherwise, remove ASCII bias
                 add    c,b          ;Add to preset value
                 inr    l            ;Point HL to next character
                 inz    h
                                     ;Check for end-of-line
cinp_1:          cpi    m,eol        character?
                 bz     cinp_2       ;If so, done and exit
                 mov    c,b          ;Multiply exisitng value by 10
                 add    c,c
                 add    c,c
                 add    c,b
                 add    c,c
                 mov    b,m          ;Get next character
                 jmp    cinp_0       ;Do again
cinp_2:          ret                 ;Return
;
;  End Program - Begin Data Section
;
data
                 Number Guessing
msg0:            Game
                 I am thinking of a
msg1:            number
msg2:            between 1 and 100.
msg3:            Your guess?
msg4:            You got it in

msg5:            tries.
msg6:            Too high.  Try again.
msg7:            Too low.  Try again.
                 Press any key to
msg8:            continue...
cr               equ                 13   ;Carriage return character
lf               equ                 10   ;Line feed character
```

```
eol              equ              10    ;End-of-line character
cntr_l           equ              12    ;Clear screen character
bs               equ               8    ;Back space character
buf_start        equ               0    ;Start of character buffer
cntr_port        equ               4    ;Terminal Unit control port
data_port        equ               5    ;Terminal Unit data port
rnd_port         equ               2    ;Randon Unit data port
;
;  End Data
Section
;
end
```

Appendix F – Conway's Game of Life

The following is listing of Conway's game of Life for the Logisim BYOC CPU:

```
;
;  Conway's
Game of Life
for Logisim
BYOC CPU
;
;  Copyright
2019 by Dick
Whipple
;
;  Set-Up
Code
;
setup:          call        clr_scr                 ;Clear screen
                                                    ;Print title
                mvi         h,hi(msg0)              message
                mvi         l,lo(msg0)
                call        mout
;
;  Copy Initial
Grid from
ROM {DE} to
RAM {HL}
;
                                                    ;Point DE to
                                                    starter grid in
                mvi         d,hi(row0)              DROM
                mvi         e,lo(row0)
                                                    ;Point HL to grid
                mvi         h,hi(grid_start_0)      0 in MRAM
```

```
                mvi     l,lo(grid_start_0)
                mvi     b,0                     ;Zero count BC
                mvi     c,0
setup_0:        lrom    a                       ;copy byte
                mov     m,a

                                                Increment HL
                inr     l                       and DE
                inz     h
                inr     e
                inz     d

                                                ;Increment
                inr     c                       count
                inz     b

                                                ;Reached end of
                cpi     c,lo(grid_size)         grid?
                                                ;If not, copy
                bnz     setup_0                 another byte
                                                ;Reached end of
                cpi     b,hi(grid_size)         grid?
                                                ;If not, copy
                bnz     setup_0                 another byte
;
; Initialize
Generation
to 0
;
                                                ;Set generation
setup_1:        mvi     a,0                     to zero
                                                ;Push it onto
                push    a                       stack
                push    a
;
; Main Code
;
main:           call    clr_scr                 ;Clear screen
```

```
                                                        ;Print title
                mvi         h,hi(msg0)                  message
                mvi         l,lo(msg0)
                call        mout
                call        print_grid                  ;Print grid 0
                                                        ;Copy grid 0 to
                call        copy_grid                   grid 1
                                                        ;Start with cell
                mvi         d,0                          (0,0); Row 0 in D
                                                        ;and column 0 in
main_0:         mvi         e,0                          E
                                                        ;Print "#" to
                                                        mark a row has
                mvi         a,35                         been scanned
                call        aout
;
;   Start cell scan of grid 1
cell (D,E)
;   Scan cells surrounding
X in this order:
;    1 2 3
;    4 X 5
;    6 7 8
;   Add 1 to A
for each live
cell
;   When
done, A
contains
number of
;   live cells
surrounding
cell X
;
```

199

```
main_1:     mvi     a,0         ;Zero A,
                                surrounding live
                                cell count
            mov     h,d         ;Start with cell
                                (D-1,E-1)
            sui     h,1
main_2:     mov     l,e
            sui     l,1

main_3:     call    scan_cells  :Check health of
                                cell
            adi     l,1         ;Increment cell
                                column
            mov     c,e         ;Continue
                                checking until
            adi     c,1         ; it is greater
                                than E+1
            cmp     c,l
            bnc     main_3

            adi     h,1         :Check health of
                                celll
                                ;Increment cell
            mov     c,d         row
                                ;Continue
            adi     c,1         checking until
                                ;until it is
                                greater than
            cmp     c,h         D+1
            bnc     main_2

                                ;A is number live
                                surrounding
;                               cells
                                ;Given A, apply
                                Life rules to cell
            call    upd_cell    in grid 1
                                ;Increment
            adi     e,1         column
```

```
            cpi      e,16              ;Last column?
            bc       main_1            ;If not, do again
                                       ;If so, increment
            adi      d,1               row
            cpi      d,16              ;Last row?
            bc       main_0            ;If not, do again
                                       ;Do for rows 0-
                                       15 and column
            jmp      main              0-15
;
; Clear
Screen
Routine
;
                                       ;Output clear
clr_scr:    mvi      a,cntr_l          sceern character
            jmp      aout
;
; Output
New Line
Routine
;
                                       ;Output end-of-
new_line:   mvi      a,eol             line character
            jmp      aout
;
; Output
Message at
HL Routine
(terminates
with 0x00)
;
mout:       push     d                 Save D
            push     e                 Save E
            mov      d,h               ;Move HL to DE
```

201

```
            mov       e,l
                                          ;Get character
mout0:      lrom      a                   at DE into B
            or        a,a                 ;Is it zero?
                                          ;If so, done and
            bz        mout_done           exit
            call      aout                ;If not, print it
            inr       e                   ;Point next DE
            inz       d
            jmp       mout0               ;Do again
mout_done:  pop       e                   ;Restore E
            pop       d                   ;Restore D
            ret                           ;Return
;
; Output
Single
Character in
A
;
aout:       push      a                   ;Save A
                                          ;Get control
aout_0:     inp       a,cntr_port         status into A
            ani       a,128               ;Is print busy?
            bnz       aout_0              ;If so, wait
            pop       a                   ;If not, output it
            out       data_port,a         ;Restore A
            ret                           ;Return
;
; Convert
Number in
DE to ASCII
and output
;
```

; L is used
as flag to
suppress
output of
leading zeros
except when
DE is zero.
;

```
deout:      push      b                ;Save B
            push      c                ;Save A
                                       ;Zero 10,000s
            mvi       l,0              counter
                                       ;Pass digit value
                                       (10000) to
                                       convert
            mvi       c,lo(10000)      subroutine
            mvi       b,hi(10000)
                                       ;Print 10,000s
            call      cnvrt            digit
                                       ;Pass digit value
                                       (1000) to
                                       convert
            mvi       c,lo(1000)       subroutine
            mvi       b,hi(1000)
                                       ;Print 1000s
            call      cnvrt            digit
                                       ;Pass digit value
                                       (100) to convert
            mvi       c,lo(100)        subroutine
            mvi       b,hi(100)
            call      cnvrt            ;Print 100s digit
                                       ;Pass digit value
                                       (10) to convert
            mvi       c,lo(10)         subroutine
            mvi       b,hi(10)
```

```
        call    cnvrt       ;Print 10s digit
                            ;Get 1s is digit in
        mov     a,e         A
        adi     a,48        ;Add ASCII bias
        call    aout        ;Print 1s digit
        pop     c           ;Restore C
        pop     b           ;Restore B
        ret                 ;Return
;
                            ;Preset H as zero
cnvrt:      mvi     h,255   surpress flag
cnvrt_0:    inr     h       ;Increment it
                            ;Subtract digit
        sub     e,c         value
        sbb     d,b
                            ;If no borow do,
        bnc     cnvrt_0     do again
                            ;If borrow, add
        add     e,c         digit value back
        adc     d,b
                            ;Is digit to be
                            printed equal to
        cmp     h,l         suppress flag?
                            ;If so, done and
        bz      cnvrt_1     exit (no print)
                            ;If not, turn off
                            zero surpress
        dcr     l           flag
                            ;Get character
        mov     a,h         to print into B
        adi     a,48        ;Add ASCII bias
        call    aout        ;Output it
cnvrt_1:    ret             ;Return
;
```

204

```
;  Copy
Grid_0 to
Grid_1
;
copy_grid:      mvi     b,0                             ;Zero counter
                                                        BC
                mvi     c,0

                                                        ;Point DE to grid
                mvi     d,hi(grid_start_0)              0 in MRAM
                mvi     e,lo(grid_start_0)
                                                        ;Point HL to grid
                mvi     h,hi(grid_start_1)              1 in MRAM
                mvi     l,lo(grid_start_1)
copy_grid_0:    lram    a                               ;Move byte
                mov     m,a

                                                        ;Increment
                inr     c                               counter
                inz     b

                                                        ;Reached end of
                cpi     c,lo(grid_size)                 grid?
                bnz     copy_grid_1                     ;If not, do again
                cpi     b,hi(grid_size)
                bnz     copy_grid_1                     ;If not, do again
                ret                                     ;Return
copy_grid_1:    inr     l                               ;Increment HL
                inz     h
                inr     e                               ;Increment DE
                inz     d
                jmp     copy_grid_0                     ;Do again
;
;   Print Grid
0
;
```

```
print_grid:      mvi      b,0              ;Zero count in
                                           BC
                 mvi      c,0

                 call     new_line         ;Print next line
                                           ;Point HL to
                 mvi      h,hi(grid_start_0)   start of grid 0
                 mvi      l,lo(grid_start_0)

                                           ;Prepare to print
print_grid_0:    mvi      a,42             asterisk
                                           ;Is cell empty
                 or       m,m              (=0)?
                                           ;If not, print
                 bnz      print_grid_1     askterisk.
                                           ;If so, print a
                 mvi      a,32             space
                                           ;Print which
print_grid_1:    call     aout             ever
                                           ;Increment
                 inr      c                count
                 inz      b

                                           ;Reached end of
                 cpi      c,lo(grid_size)  grid?
                 bnz      print_grid_2     ;If not, move on
                 cpi      b,hi(grid_size)
                 bnz      print_grid_2     ;If not, move on
                                           ;If so, new line
                                           and print
                 call     new_line         generation
                                           ;Print
                 mvi      h,hi(msg1)        generation title
                 mvi      l,lo(msg1)
                 call     mout

                                           ;Get generation
                                           number off
                 pop      e                stack
```

206

```
                pop        d
                inr        e                        ;Increment it
                inz        d
                                                    ;Put back on
                push       d                        stack
                push       e
                call       deout                    ;Print it
                                                    ;Print a space
                mvi        a,space                  and return
                jmp        aout
print_grid_2:   mov        a,c                      ;At end of row?
                ani        a,15
                bnz        print_grid_3             ;If not, move on
                call       new_line                 ;If so, next line
print_grid_3:   inr        l                        ;Point next cell
                inz        h
                jmp        print_grid_0             ;Do over
;
; Calculate
A, the
number of
living cells
;
surrounding
the cell(D,E)
;
                                                    ;Is this the
scan_cells:     cmp        h,d                      cell(d,e)?
                bnz        scan_cells_0             ;If not, continue
                                                    ;Is this the
                cmp        l,e                      cell(d,e)?
                bnz        scan_cells_0             ;If not, continue
                                                    ;If so, do
                                                    nothing and
                ret                                 return
```

```
;
;  The code below creates a torus grid. When
;  a cell is off the grid on one edge, the
;  cell on the opposie edge is checked instead.
;
scan_cells_0:    mov        b,h
                 adi        b,16
                 mov        c,l
                 cpi        b,16
                 bnc        scan_cells_1
                 mvi        b,31
scan_cells_1:    cpi        b,32
                 bc         scan_cells_2
                 mvi        b,16
scan_cells_2:    cpi        l,128
                 bc         scan_cells_3
                 mvi        c,15
                 jmp        scan_cells_4
scan_cells_3:    cpi        l,16
                 bc         scan_cells_4
                 mvi        c,0
;
```

; Calculate the address of the cell(B,C)
;

```
scan_cells_4:    push      h          Save HL
                 push      l

                                      ;Multiply the
                 mvi       h,0        row by 16
                 mov       l,b
                 rlc       l          ; By 2
                 ral       h

                                      ;By 2 again (now
                 rlc       l          4)
                 ral       h

                                      ;By 2 again (now
                 rlc       l          8)
                 ral       h

                                      ;By 2 again (now
                 rlc       l          16)
                 ral       h

                                      ;Add column; HL
                                      is now address
                 add       l,c        of probed cell
                                      ;Add the value
                                      in cell (either 1
                 add       a,m        or 0) to A
                 pop       l          ;Restore HL
                 pop       h

                 ret                  ;Return
```

;
; Update cel(D,E) based on A (number of

live neighbor
cells)
;

```
                                                            ;Get the cell's
upd_cell:       call        get_cell_adrs                   address
                cpi         m,0                             ;Is it dead (=0)?
                bnz         upd_cell_0                      ;If not, continue
                                                            ;If so,has it
                                                            exactly 3
                cpi         a,3                             neighbors?
                bnz         upd_cell_0                      ;If not, continue
                                                            ;If so, change
                mvi         m,1                             cell to live
                ret                                         ;Return
                                                            ;2 or more
                                                            occupied cells
upd_cell_0:     cpi         a,2                             around it?
                bnc         upd_cell_1                      ;If so, continue
                                                            ;If not, cell dies
                                                            of
                                                            underpoplulatio
                mvi         m,0                             n
                ret                                         ;Return
                                                            ;Cell has 2 or 3
upd_cell_1:     cpi         a,4                             neighbors?
                                                            ;If so, leave alive
                bc          upd_cell_2                      and exit
                                                            ;If 4 or more,
                                                            cell dies of
                mvi         m,0                             overcrowding
upd_cell_2:     ret                                         ;Return
;
;  Get
cell(D,E)
```

```
                                               address into
                                               HL
                                               ;
get_cell_adrs                                  ;Multiply the
:              mvi      h,0                     row in D by 16
               mov      l,d
               rlc      l                       ;By 2
               ral      h

                                               ;By 2 again (4
               rlc      l                       now)
               ral      h

                                               ;By 2 again (8
               rlc      l                       now)
               ral      h

                                               ;By 2 again (16
               rlc      l                       now)
               ral      h

                                               ;Add column in
               add      l,e                     E
               ret                              ;Return
;
; End
Program -
Begin Data
Section
;
data
;
; Program
Equates
;
grid_size      equ                        256  ;Grid size
                                               ;Carriage return
cr             equ                         13  character
```

```
                                            ;Line feed
lf          equ                        10   character
                                            ;End-of-line
eol         equ                        10   character
                                            ;Clear screen
cntr_l      equ                        12   character
space       equ                        32   ;space character
                                            ;Backspace
bs          equ                         8   character
                                            ;Terminal Unit
cntr_port   equ                         4   control port
                                            ;Terminal Unit
data_port   equ                         5   data port
;
;  Data ROM
;
; Starter Grid
;
                        1,0,0,0,0,0,0,0,0,0,0,0,0,0,0
row0:       db          ,1
                        0,0,0,0,0,0,0,0,0,0,0,0,0,0,0
            db          ,0
                        0,0,0,0,0,0,0,0,0,0,0,0,0,0,0
            db          ,0
                        0,0,0,0,0,0,0,0,0,0,0,0,0,0,0
            db          ,0
                        0,0,0,0,0,0,0,0,0,0,0,0,0,0,0
            db          ,0
                        0,0,0,0,0,0,0,1,0,0,0,0,0,0,0
            db          ,0
                        0,0,0,0,0,0,1,1,1,0,0,0,0,0,0
            db          ,0
                        0,0,0,0,0,0,1,0,1,0,0,0,0,0,0
            db          ,0
                        0,0,0,0,0,0,1,1,1,0,0,0,0,0,0
            db          ,0
```

```
                          0,0,0,0,0,0,0,1,0,0,0,0,0,0,0
              db          ,0
                          0,0,0,0,0,0,0,0,0,0,0,0,0,0,0
              db          ,0
                          0,0,0,0,0,0,0,0,0,0,0,0,0,0,0
              db          ,0
                          0,0,0,0,0,0,0,0,0,0,0,0,0,0,0
              db          ,0
                          0,0,0,0,0,0,0,0,0,0,0,0,0,0,0
              db          ,0
                          0,0,0,0,0,0,0,0,0,0,0,0,0,0,0
              db          ,0
                          1,0,0,0,0,0,0,0,0,0,0,0,0,0,0
              db          ,1
;
              Conway's
              Game of
msg0:         Life
msg1:         Gen
              Press any
              key to
              continue
msg8:         ...
;
;  Data RAM
Map
;
ram_start     equ                                   0
grid_start_0  equ                                   0
grid_start_1  equ          grid_start_0 + grid_size
;
;  End Data
Section
;
end
```

Appendix G – ZOC PC Terminal Emulator

The ZOC Terminal Emulator can be downloaded from here[10]. Terminal emulators transmit PC keystrokes to the BYOC CPU via GX Starter Board's USB Data Port and displays information from the CPU on a PC window. After installing and launching the ZOC Terminal Emulator, the starter page will appear. Click on File.

Choose Quick Connection to see this screen:

---

[10] https://www.emtec.com/zoc/terminal-emulator.html

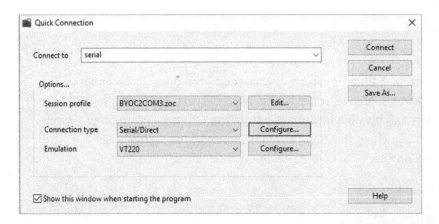

Select Serial Direct as the Connection Type and VT220 as the Emulation. Then click Edit...

Lastly, while I subscribe to English physicist and electrical engineer Oliver Heaviside's dictum, "Should I refuse a good dinner simply because I do not understand the process of digestion?", I do say the knowing how it was made and the choice of ingredients makes for the great eating pleasure

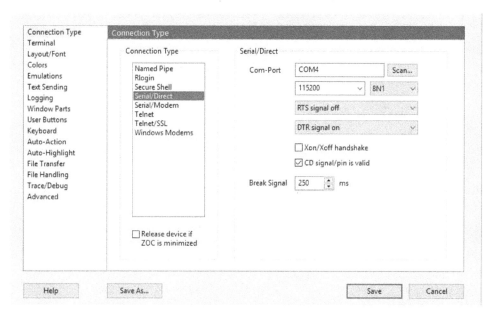

Click Scan to find and select the communication port connected to the G5 Starter Board USB Data Port. Some experimentation may be needed here. Also, be sure that only the USB Data Port is connected. The Data and Blaster USB cannot both be connected at the same time. Now select 155200 (serial data rate), 8N1 (8-bit data word with 1 stop bit), CD signal/pin s valid, and Break Signal 250 ms. Click Save As and give the Session Profile a name.

At this point, the Quick Connection screen will reappear. Click Connect and the logon screen should appear.

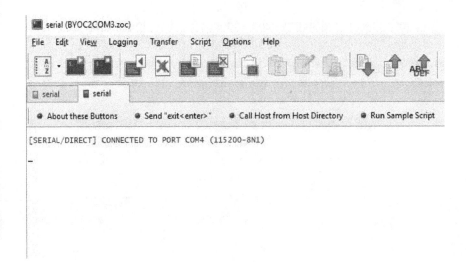

The terminal emulator is ready to communicate with the BYOC CPU.

www.ingramcontent.com/pod-product-compliance
Lightning Source LLC
Chambersburg PA
CBHW031219050326
40689CB00009B/1390